The GREAT Book of
TRANSPORT

The complete guide to land, air and sea transportation

www.alligatorbooks.co.uk

© 2006 Alligator Books Limited

Published by
Alligator Books Limited
Gadd House, Arcadia Avenue
London N3 2JU

Written by Lynne Gibbs
Printed in China

This volume was previously published as six separate titles in the *Mega Book of* series:
Trains; *Ships*; *Motorcycles*; *Cars*; *Trucks*; *Aircraft*.

PICTURE CREDITS
T=top; B=bottom; C=centre

CONTENTS

Introduction 4

Trains 6

Ships 34

Motorcycles 56

Cars 78

Trucks 102

Aircraft 126

Glossary 154

Index 158

The earliest form of transportation was the horse. But this was often a slow, tiring and uncomfortable way to get around. Then along came the horse-drawn cart and carriage. This revolutionized travel because it enabled groups of people and their belongings to move together. But it was still a slow mode of transportation and could only be used to travel short distances.

Long-distance travel

For hundreds of years, ships were the only form of transportation available for travelling long distances. They were used to discover foreign lands. By Victorian times, ships carried large numbers of people across the world. Most passengers travelled in basic, unhygienic quarters. This made long journeys unsafe and many people died.

Over-land travel

In the last hundred years, with the invention of the steam engine, we have achieved many ways to travel in comfort, style

– and at high speeds. Ships, although still used to carry cargo, are now primarily used by passengers as luxury cruise and holiday vessels. Since the 1800s, trains have been used to transport passengers and cargo all over the world, and across remote deserts. For travelling short distances, between towns and in cities for example, cars, trucks and motorcycles are still the most favoured means of getting around.

Taking to the skies

With the invention of aircraft, travelling changed forever! The latest supersonic jets, capable of travelling faster than the speed of sound, are now able to take us from one side of the world to the other in a matter of hours. Inside **The Great Book of Transport** you can learn more about some of the most important, outstanding and unique forms of transportation during the last hundred years.

TRAINS

Although they provided a good service, the early steam trains polluted the air with their thick, billowing smoke. Modern diesel and electric trains are much cleaner, more efficient and a great deal faster!

THE TRAIN CLOSE-UP

Locomotives took off in the early 1800s. At this time, engines were powered by steam made from water heated by coal fires. On the following pages you can read about some of the greatest locomotives in history – from the first steam trains to hit the tracks, to the fastest and strangest in design and technology.

FORCE OF GRAVITY

The first railways were built in Europe over 250 years ago. They were used to carry coal from mines, loaded wagons or chaldrons. They could only run downhill on flat stone laid in the ground. Metal rails soon followed. The wheels had projecting rims (flanges) on either side to stop trucks from running off the tracks.

MEGA FACT
Built in 1960, Evening Star was the last steam locomotive built for British Rail. It was used for freight work and to pull passenger and express trains.

How a steam engine works

The diagram shows the inside of an 1840s locomotive. Burning coal in the fire box heats air in the boiler tubes, which boil water in the boiler. This creates steam, which collects in the dome. The driver can open a valve to let steam pass through the steam pipe and push pistons backwards and forwards. The pistons are connected by rods to the driving wheels and make them turn. The pistons also push exhaust steam up the blast pipe and out through the chimney. This draws the hot air from the fire box and helps the fire to burn well.

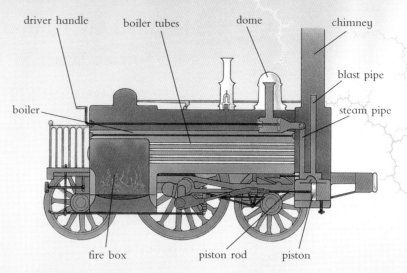

driver handle   boiler tubes   dome   chimney

boiler

blast pipe

steam pipe

fire box   piston rod   piston

MEGA FACT
Until the early 1900s, horse-drawn railways were used throughout the world to pull vehicles for both passengers and freight.

AT YOUR CONVENIENCE

Until 1882, passengers had to stay in one compartment until the train stopped, as there was no passageway for them to move from one compartment to another. In that year, cars with a side aisle came into service. At each end of the aisle was a bathroom — one for ladies, the other strictly for gentlemen!

TRAINS TAKE TO THE TRACKS

Since the first practical steam engines were designed by Thomas Newcomen in 1712, and James Watt in 1769, engineers had tried to use steam power to drive a self-propelled vehicle. It was in the early 1800s that the first successful guided railway locomotives were designed and built. In 1823, George and his son Robert Stephenson set up the world's first locomotive works in Newcastle-upon-Tyne, England. It built steam engines that were sold all over the world.

MEGA FACT
Until 1896, the speed limit for cars in Britain was just 3.2 km/h — that's the average person's walking pace!

Trevithick's steam locomotive

Richard Trevithick, from Cornwall, England, designed the first steam locomotive in 1804. It ran on rails for the South Wales Pen-y-Darren Iron Works. The locomotive was adapted from a stationary steam engine and was so heavy, that it shattered the tracks. This little 'mishap' delayed rail travel technology for another 20 years.

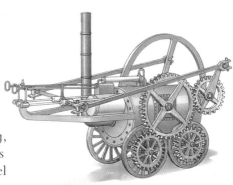

ROCKET RACES AWAY

In 1829, a group of British businessmen decided to build a railroad between Manchester and Liverpool. They could not decide whether to use horse-drawn carriages or cars pulled by a steam locomotive, so they announced a competition for anyone who could produce a reliable steam engine. Robert Stephenson built and entered the Rocket. This steam engine carried its own coal and water to make the steam that drove its wheels in a railcar behind the driver. The Rocket achieved a world speed record of 58 km/h, which was amazingly fast for its time.

MEGA FACT

In 1769, Frenchman Nicholas Cugnot built the first self-propelled vehicle in the world. But the three-wheeled steam-powered road vehicle was difficult to control and the project was abandoned.

STEPHENSON'S ROCKET

After the success of the Rocket, steam-powered locomotives developed rapidly and the railway industry expanded. The world's first railway trains steamed along in Britain, but soon many countries began to develop their own railway systems. As well as providing better and cheaper transport, rail travel created thousands of jobs.

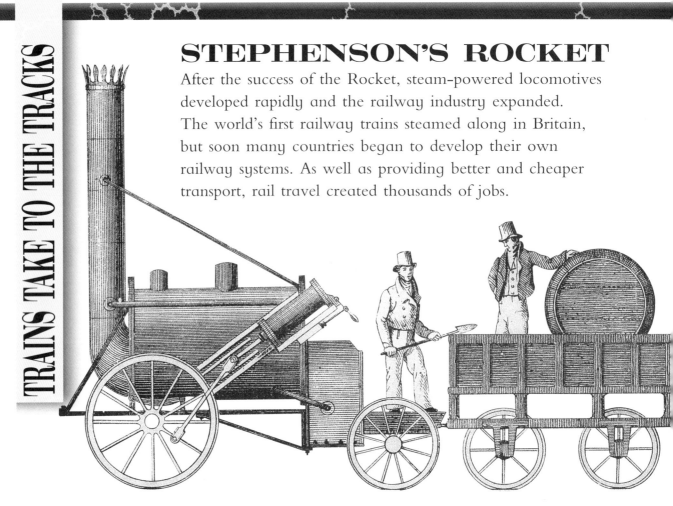

STIRLING 8ft SINGLE CLASS 4-2-2

Patrick Stirling, superintendent of England's Great Northern Railway, had the first Stirling Single built in 1870 at the line's own Doncaster Locomotive Plant. Its elegant lines, gleaming paint-work and polished brass trim make it one of the most beautiful engines ever made. The huge 2.4 metre-driving wheels allowed the engines to reach very high speeds. The engine had outside cylinders but inside valve chests – the slide valves being driven direct by sets of Stephenson's link motion.

When the driver pulled the brake lever, a vacuum was created in the brake pipe. This pushed the brake shoes onto the wheels and stopped the train.

Best Friend of Charleston

The first full-size steam locomotive to be built in North America went into service on 15 January 1831. Constructed at the West Point Foundry in New York, Best Friend of Charleston ran on the South Carolina Railroad, North America's first commercial steam railway. Best Friend of Charleston travelled at 32 km/h. It handled a five-car train and carried over 50 passengers.

PUFFING BILLY

Puffing Billy was the first locomotive to operate commercially as a train using the idea of a smooth wheel on a smooth rail. It was built in 1813 by William Hedley to haul loaded coal wagons at about 7 km/h from Wylam Colliery in Northumberland, England, to the River Tyne – a distance of 8 km. The track was damaged by the locomotive's weight and had to be rebuilt. Because complaints were made about the noise and smoke that it made, Puffing Billy was modified so that the steam passed through a 'quieting' chamber before going up the chimney.

MEGA FACT
Because of the plentiful supply of coal, and to ease road traffic congestion, steam engines are still used in China today.

FLYING SCOTSMAN

In 1923, Flying Scotsman was the first express passenger locomotive to be built by the then newly formed London and North-Eastern Railway. In 1934, Flying Scotsman was the first steam locomotive to achieve a speed of 160 km/h. British Railways withdrew the world-famous locomotive from service in 1963. Over 70 similar locomotives were scrapped, leaving Flying Scotsman the sole survivor of its class. In 1977, the locomotive co-starred in the film *Agatha* with Dustin Hoffman. Then in 1966, it was sold for a staggering £1,250,000. A further £750.000 was spent rebuilding the classic to its former glory.

RM CLASS 4-6-2

China's RM Class 4-6-2 is thought to be the last steam express passenger locomotive in the world. Construction of the RM (Ren Ming) class began in 1958 at the Szufang (Tsing-tao) Works. The main difference between the RM Class and almost all other steam engines was the position of the main steam-pipe. This normally ran forward from the dome inside the boiler, but in these engines there was enough room for it to be placed inside insulated trunking above the boiler.

MEGA FACT
Isambard Kingdom Brunel (1806-1859) designed many of Britain's great railways, bridges and tunnels.

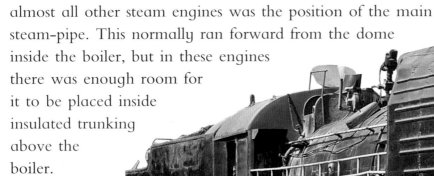

Turbomotive 4-6-2

Turbine engines had been used for many years to power ships and electric generators, but they had not been widely used for locomotives. In 1932 William Stanier, Chief Mechanical Engineer of the London Midland & Scottish Railway, built a turbine locomotive to carry out propulsion experiments. The Turbomotive 4-6-2 gave 500,000 kilometres of service. It looked promising, but there were problems. In 1951, following a failure of the main turbine, the express passenger locomotive was rebuilt into a normal 4-6-2 and named Princess Anne.

BIG BOY

Union Pacific's 500-tonne Big Boy is the world's largest, most powerful steam locomotive ever built. The engines were built in the 1940s to haul heavy freight trains uphill in Utah, USA. Before Big Boy, a helper service was needed. Big Boys could reach speeds of up to 130 km/h, but produced a maximum continuous power of 113 km/h. Only twenty-five were built. The first group, 'class 1', was built in 1941 and numbered 4000-4019. The second group, 'class 2', was built in 1944 and numbered 4020-4024. The last revenue freight pulled by a Big Boy was in 1959.

MEGA FACT

In the 1840s, wealthy people travelled in their own covered carriages. The poor had to sit in open trucks. By 1850, railways provided covered carriages for all travellers.

DIESEL AND ELECTRIC LOCOS

The invention of diesel-powered and electric locomotives brought the age of steam to a close. Diesel-powered trains are often used on lines that are not busy, and where electrification of rails is not economical. The first electric trains were developed at the end of the 19th century. After World War II, many countries in Europe rebuilt their damaged railway systems by electrifying old lines as well as building new ones.

MEGA FACT
German engineer Dr Rudolph Diesel demonstrated the first diesel engine in 1897.

DIESEL VERSUS ELECTRIC
Electric locomotives are faster, quieter, easier to run than diesel, and do not emit smoke. There are more moving parts in a diesel engine than in an electric engine, so friction is higher.

Inside a diesel-electric locomotive

Diesel oil burns with explosive force in cylinders in the engine. This drives pistons that in turn drive a generator, which makes electricity. The generator powers the traction motors that turn the locomotive's wheels. Extra electricity is stored in batteries. The radiator keeps the diesel engine cool, and the exhaust lets out used gases. Diesel engines are more efficient and smoother than steam locos, so do less damage to the railway track.

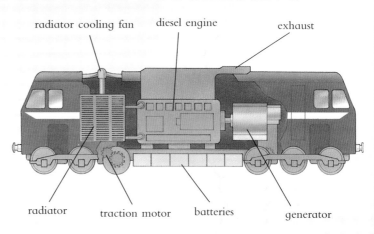

radiator cooling fan   diesel engine   exhaust

radiator   traction motor   batteries   generator

BIG, BOLD AND BEAUTIFUL

In 1969 the Union Pacific Railroad, known for its large steam locos, purchased the largest and most powerful diesel engine ever built – the DDA40X. Named Centennial, these 270-tonne, 29 metre-long beasts were powered by two engines providing 6,600hp. In all, 47 units numbered 6900-6946 were purchased. Centennials were designed for high-speed freight and by 1980 had averaged 3 million kilometres a piece. Like the Big Boys, 113 km/h was attainable with heavy tonnage trains on level track.

INTERCITY 125

The Intercity 125 diesel-electric high-speed train is common along main lines in the UK. An Intercity 125 is made up of two 'class 43' power cars, one at each end, and seven or eight passenger trailers in the middle. Being diesel engines, they are not particularly powerful, generating only 2250hp. This is why two of them are needed for high speeds. Australian rail based their high-speed XPT on the 'class 43' power cars, although the XPT is not as fast as its British counterpart.

Flying Hamburger

With its striking mauve and cream gleaming livery, the German-built Fliegender Hamburger (Flying Hamburger) set off on its first journey from Berlin to Hamburg on 15 May 1933, travelling at 124.5 km/h. The Flying Hamburger was a two-car, articulated diesel unit with a 410hp engine mounted on each end bogie. There was accommodation for 98 second-class passengers in the two coaches and four seats at the small buffet.

Eurotram

Tramways were built throughout Europe after World War II. Many of the lines have now disappeared, yet trams remain one of the most efficient ways of moving people efficiently, especially in heavily populated cities. In 1994 the Eurotram, built by ABB Transportation, came into service in Strasbourg, France. Operating on an entirely new system, it runs on reserved track, in tunnels or in streets, and has a maximum speed of 21 km/h.

CENTENNIAL

Centennials were designed to operate over all the Union Pacific main lines in the USA. The Centennial design was unique to Union Pacific, but it incorporated many of the best features of other up-to-date American locomotives. With the decline of freight transport, Centennials were taken out of circulation in 1980. During the economic recovery of 1984, 25 Centennials were then returned to service. But due to their high maintenance costs, most of these well-loved locomotives were retired again by 1986.

MEGA FACT
There are nearly 18,000 km of track on the British railway system.

MEGA FACT
The electric tramway in Blackpool, England, is one of only three systems in the world to use double-deck cars.

DIESEL AND ELECTRIC LOCOS

DELTIC

Otherwise known as the 'class 55', the Deltic was built in 1961-62 by English Electric. It became one of the most powerful diesel-electric single-unit locomotives in the world, replacing the Mallard-type steam locomotives. It weighed a mighty 99 tonnes and had a maximum speed of 160 km/h. With a brake force of 51 tonnes, the locomotive's speed record was 182 km/h. In the 20 years that the Deltics worked the East Coast line between London and Edinburgh, they each ran more than five million kilometres.

MEGA FACT
In 1879, the first practical electric railway was demonstrated at an exhibition in Berlin. Designed and operated by German engineer Werner von Siemens, the locomotive travelled at 6.5 km/h and pulled 30 passengers.

RAILWAYS UNDERGROUND

The world's first underground railway was built in London, England, in 1863. A steam-powered railway ran just below the streets and connected the main line stations of Paddington to Farringdon Street. Until the installation of electric-powered trains in 1890, the 'tubes' – as they became known – were often smokey and hot. But they were quicker and more convenient than travelling by road. By the end of the 19th century other cities around the world began building their own underground railways.

Northern line

51534

MEGA FACT
One large passenger train can carry the same number of people as 100 cars.

Docklands Light Railway (DLR)

Light rail transit systems such as the DLR in London, provide an easy way to travel in a busy city. The DLR, installed in the Docklands in 1984-87, was designed to carry 2,000 passengers an hour in single cars. It became so popular that the system was rebuilt with multiple-unit trains to carry up to 12,000 passengers an hour. These 'driverless' trains are powered by electricity collected from a 'third rail' along the track, and are operated automatically by computer from a central control room.

CLASS 58

This powerful diesel-electric freight locomotive has a 3,300hp, 12-cylinder engine. It is capable of hauling 1,000 tonnes on the level at 129 km/h and was built to cope with the expected increase in coal traffic due to an oil crisis. The 'class 58' was built in Romania and delivered to British Railways in 1982. The main advantage of these locos was that the self-contained cabs could be disconnected, unbolted and replaced quickly. It often took months to repair a damaged cab on earlier British Rail diesels.

MEGA FACT
Electro-diesels require less servicing than diesel-electric trains, and have better acceleration. They also run more smoothly at high speed, which causes less wear.

RECORD BREAKERS

Since the first steam trains, railways have always tried to make and break speed records. For Britain and the USA, breaking the speed barrier of 160 km/h was the first achievement. An American locomotive was claimed to have reached a speed of 181 km/h in 1893, but this was never officially recognised. With new technology, attempts to beat new rail speed records will continue.

MEGA FACT
Trans-Siberian Express The Russia, makes the longest regular passenger train journey in the world. It travels 9,297 km, between Moscow and Vladivostock, and takes eight days to complete the journey.

RACING ALONG THE RAILS

Owned and operated by SNCF, the French national railway, the TGV (Train à Grande Vitesse), is an electric train that runs between Paris and Lyon. For much of this route, the TGV runs on a special track at around 212 km/h. Its top speed is 300 km/h, although a modified TGV set a world record in 1990 when it reached 515.3 km/h in trial runs. The TGV was developed as a high-speed system that was also compatible with the existing railway infrastructure where building new tracks or stations would have been too expensive.

Mail on the move

Until 1838, special mail coaches had delivered the Royal Mail. With the development of the railway passenger service in Britain, it was thought that a faster and more efficient service could be provided by rail. The travelling 'post office van' handled all the jobs that were carried out by a normal post office. It automatically picked up mail from specially designed lineside apparatus while still moving. After being sorted and put into sacks for different destinations along the route, the sacks were automatically dropped off into lineside nets. Railways are still used today by mail services, along with road and air transport.

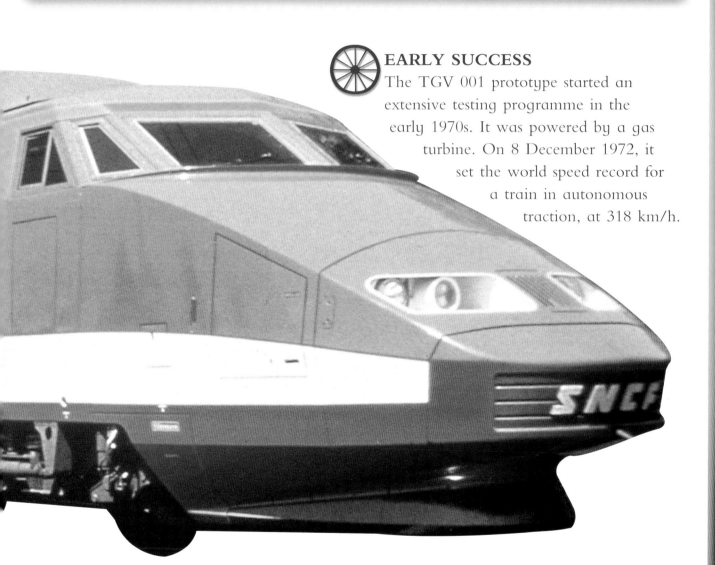

EARLY SUCCESS

The TGV 001 prototype started an extensive testing programme in the early 1970s. It was powered by a gas turbine. On 8 December 1972, it set the world speed record for a train in autonomous traction, at 318 km/h.

DOUBLE DECKER

The TGV Duplex was designed to maximise the number of people carried in one group of rail cars, or trainsets. Its two seating levels can carry 545 passengers. The TGV Duplex is poised to become the busiest of the TGV fleet as orders for additional trainsets mount.

MEGA FACT
Most diesel engines power a generator, which makes electricity. This drives a motor that turns the wheels.

RECORD BREAKERS

TGV – TRAIN À GRANDE VITESSE

There is actually no such thing as the TGV and there are many big differences among the 350 or more of these trainsets in service today. The name 'TGV' refers to more than just the trains. It is a whole system, comprising of the train, the track and signalling technologies that, when combined, make high speeds possible. Almost all TGVs are made of steel. Weight-saving features on the newest models, such as the TGV Duplex, include aluminium body shells and magnesium seat frames.

THE ICE

German InterCity Express (ICE) trains began public service in 1991, running from Hamburg to Munich via Frankfurt. The trains run mainly on upgraded existing lines, although special high-speed tracks are also used. During tests on these lines, the ICE set a German high-speed record of 404 km/h, which held the world record for a short time.

X-2000 TILTING EXPRESS

Sweden's hilly countryside has made the building of new railway lines expensive, so they came up with the 'tilting' train. By 1990, the first twenty X-2000 tilting express trains, with a maximum speed of 210 km/h, were in operation. The tilting mechanism on these trains is controlled by an accelerometer at the front of the train. The degree of 'tilt' is limited to an amount where a passenger sitting on a corner seat on one side of a coach is no more than 300 mm higher or lower than a passenger on the other side.

MEGA FACT
The Hiawatha Express was the fastest scheduled steam train to ever run.

PACIFIC MALLARD

Designed by British engineer Sir Nigel Gresley, the Mallard set a world speed record for a steam locomotive on 3 July 1938. Primarily on a special run to test braking, it achieved a speed of 203 km/h on the descent of Stoke Bank between Grantham in Lincolnshire and Peterborough in Cambridgeshire, England. This record still stands, over 60 years later.

REACHING FOR THE SKY

Some rail systems run on or hang underneath rails attached to overhead structures. Overhead railways are relatively cheap to build and help to free ground space. There are two types. Suspended railways have trains hanging under the rail, with wheels that are fitted onto the rails. 'Straddle' railways are where a train fits over a single rail. Trains running on the 'straddle' system rest astride the rail and are guided by panels on either side of the rail. Overhead systems with a single rail are called 'monorails'.

NOT SO NEW
Overhead railways are not new. They are operated like any bus, heavy metro or conventional railway system. The Wuppertal, in Germany, was built in 1901. Wheel carriages hang from a single rail and are electrically driven.

VERSATILE TRAVEL
Overhead rail systems are an efficient way to travel in congested cities, around theme parks – and skiers often use a monorail to travel from one mountain peak to another.

MEGA FACT
In 1888, Granville Woods designed and patented a system for overhead electric conducting lines for railroads. This contributed to the development of the overhead railroad system found in cities such as New York, USA.

MEGA FACT
A goods train can carry the same amount of goods as 50 lorries.

IS IT A PLANE?

In 1929, Scottish engineer George Bennie built a suspended monorail that travelled at 160 km/h along a track using electric propellers. There were plans for a high-speed link between London and Paris, with a seaplane (Railplane) to carry passengers across the English Channel. Due to the world economic depression of the 1930s, the project did not progress past the experimental stage.

REACHING FOR THE SKY

WUPPERTAL SCHWEBEBAHN

Designed by German engineer Eugen Langen, the Wuppertal Schwebebahn (swinging railway) has been in service since 1901. The entire system required over 19,000 tonnes of steel, with 472 steel supports carrying the track. By 1990, 16.7 million passengers a year were travelling on the Schwebebahn. The electric trains travel at 26.5 km/h, although their top speed is 60 km/h. For most of the 12.9 km journey, the railway straddles the river Wupper.

MEGA FACT

The longest cableway in the world, between Boliden and Kristineberg in Sweden, was built in 1942 — and runs for 96 km!

FUNICULAR RAILWAY

A funicular railway uses the technology of an elevator (a cable pulling a car up) and that of a railroad (a car on a track). A conventional train cannot travel up a steep incline because the steel train wheels do not have enough traction against steel rails. The funicular overcomes this by pulling the 'car' up by a cable. The wheels are only to guide the car. Funiculars use two cars at the same time, one on each side of the top pulley — one car balancing the weight of the other. The descending car's weight helps pull the ascending car up the mountain, and the ascending train keeps the speed of the descending train from going out of control. Funiculars have also been built for travel into caves and mines.

Elevated railway

Completed in 1870, New York's elevated railway was the first urban rapid transit system to be built in the USA. The need to move people between business districts and residential areas in Manhattan encouraged the development of alternative travel forms to road vehicles. Although the 'El' helped dissolve some of New York's street crowds, mechanical problems made the system unpopular for almost a decade. The steam locomotives pulling the wooden passenger cars were noisy and caused nearby buildings to shake. Walkers below the track also risked being hit by falling ash or oil.

MEGA FACT
The Qinghai-Tibet Railway in China is the highest — and longest in the world. When completed, the longest tunnel on the railway will be 1,142 km long.

MONORAIL

Many of today's theme parks have their own specially built monorail systems. These monorails vary in size and style, but their basic purpose is to transport passengers. A large dual-rail system was built at Walt Disney World in Florida, USA, in 1975. The Tokyo/Haneda Monorail, built in Japan in 1964, was the first major system to use switches for direction reversal.

LATEST LOCOS

Today, fast, cheap flights and modern road transportation seem to be winning the war for carrying freight and passengers. Trains are often, though not always, seen as noisy, uncomfortable and crowded. But concerns about pollution and road congestion has lead to a renewed interest in trains. The latest trains are brighter, faster – and technologically more sophisticated.

MEGA FACT
The Channel Tunnel, opened in 1994, stretches for 33 km beneath the English Channel that separates France from England.

MAGNETIC PROPULSION

Maglev trains give passengers a very smooth, quiet ride. 'Maglev' is short for magnetic levitation. By using magnets to replace the traditional steel wheel and track trains, maglev trains are able to 'float' on a cushion of air above a metal track. This technique eliminates friction. The lack of friction and the train's aerodynamics allow the vehicle to reach super speeds of 500 km/h. Long-distance maglev services may well be the trains of the future, but today the tracks are still considered very expensive to build.

How a maglev train works

The maglev runs in a guideway, (a trenchlike track). There are magnets in the guideway and on the train. Magnets on the floor of the guideway repel the train's magnets, lifting it up 10 cm. Magnets on the sides of the guideway and on the train alternately attract and repel each other, pushing the train along.

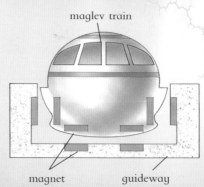

maglev train

magnet   guideway

AIRPORT TRAINS

A rapid transport system has been successfully used in airports in Britain and the USA to transport people to and from different terminals. Travelling at speeds of up to 41 km/h, the trains run on rubber tyres along a concrete track and are guided by a central steel rail.

WHAT, NO WHEELS?

Maglevs travel on magnetic tracks called guideways. These sometimes have high sides to help them guide the train. As the train does not touch the guideway, there are no moving parts, such as wheels, to wear out. Instead of engines, magnets in the track ahead of the train attract it forward and magnets behind help push the train on.

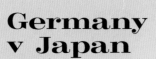

LATEST LOCOS

EUROSTAR

Eurostar adopted the basic principles used in the French TGV. The designers, however, made some important changes to the Eurostar. The main change was that it had to be able to operate in different countries. This meant that it had to be capable of using the electrical supply from three different systems, including current collection from a third rail in Britain. Operating from London between Paris and Brussels via the Channel Tunnel, Eurostar passenger trains have their own police and customs on board, as well as a prison compartment!

Germany v Japan

Although they are based on similar concepts, the German and Japanese maglev trains have major differences. In Germany, engineers are building an electromagnetic suspension (EMS) system called 'Transrapid'. In this system, the bottom of the train wraps around a magnetised coil running along the track. Electromagnets attached to the train's undercarriage are directed up toward the guideway. This levitates the train about 1 cm above the guideway and keeps the train levitated even when it is not moving. The Japanese use an electrodynamic suspension (EDS) system for their version of the maglev (shown here), which is based on the repelling force of magnets.

SHINKANSEN

In the mid-1960s, Japan began a high-speed rail service between Tokyo and Osaka. The Shinkansen trains sped along at around 217 km/h. Today, a 16-car Shinkansen, which is Japanese for 'new main line', can reach speeds of more than 268 km/h. These locomotives became known as 'bullet' trains because of their sleek design. Apart from the original 3-abreast seats still fitted to some '0' and '200' series trains, all the seats in a Shinkansen car can be rotated either to face the direction of travel or to form bays of facing seats. The typical service life of a Shinkansen train is about 15 to 20 years.

VIRGIN'S PENDOLINO

A concept based on the way a motorcyclist combats centrifugal forces by leaning into a bend, was behind the technology of the 'tilting' train. In 2002, London's Euston station was the venue for the first public showing of Virgin's Pendolino tilting train. The Pendolino is also running successfully in Italy, Germany, Spain and Switzerland. Each train has been designed to run at speeds of up to 225 km/h. The train's tilt enables it to negotiate bends at far greater speeds than conventional trains.

SHIPS

With the invention of aircraft, especially since the 1950s, travelling by ship has decreased. Today, ships are used for luxury cruises but they are also the main method for transporting cargo around the world.

THE MODERN SHIP

Since the wooden trading boats of the Ancient Egyptians, ships have been the main mode of travel across rivers and seas. The Phoenicians (an ancient people of modern-day Lebanon and Syria) developed the galley, powered by oar and sail, the Ancient Greeks and Romans used their ships to trade around the Mediterranean, the Vikings explored the north Atlantic in longboats and the Chinese carried cargo in their ships' hulls. From the early steamships to the latest liners, ships have become bigger, faster and more reliable than ever before. Over the following pages, you will discover how some of the greatest modern ships have changed the history of sea-going vessels.

MEGA FACT
In 1794, England's Earl of Stanhope built a steam-powered vessel named The Kent. *This was an experimental ship, which though not successful, led to the development of vessels that were a success.*

FROM SAIL TO STEAM

During the reign of Queen Victoria, Britain was one of the world's leading industrial nations. As an island, most of her wealth depended on her merchant ships, which carried people and goods around her huge empire. British ships had to be among the best in the world, and using steam for propelling ships through the water was a great advantage.

How a diesel engine works

Diesel engines are used to power anything from small machines to huge ships. All diesel engines work on the same principle, but they vary in size. A diesel engine, which has no spark plug, takes in air, compresses it and then injects fuel directly into the compressed air. The heat of the compressed air lights the fuel spontaneously.

■ Fuel oil

□ Lubricating oil

■ Exhaust gas

□ Jacket water

■ Sea/fresh water

□ Starting air

□ Scavenge air

SYMPHONY

MEGA BRIGHT

American inventor Thomas Alva Edison (1847–1931) created the forerunner of the gramophone, the first electric filament bulb, the radio tube and a method of telegraphic messaging between moving ships and trains. Yet he had only three months' official schooling in his life!

EVERYTHING YOU NEED!

With passenger capacities ranging from 400 to 3,000 people, standard cruise ships are categorised by their size, number of cabins and onboard amenities. Onboard characteristics vary from ship to ship. Designed to be self-contained floating resorts, cruise ships need to be capable of spending several days or more at sea.

MEGA FACT

Dug out of the sandy desert, the Suez Canal allows ships to travel from the Mediterranean to the Red Sea instead of going all the way around Africa.

LINERS AND CRUISE SHIPS

In the early 20th century, huge liners carried hundreds of people across vast oceans. While third class (steerage) passengers lived in basic, overcrowded conditions, first class ticket holders travelled in luxury. But by the mid 1960s, as air travel became cheaper and faster, ocean liners were soon replaced by cruise liners. Today, with every possible facility onboard, passengers often only go ashore to see the sights as the ship makes short stops in different countries.

MEGA FACT
The Chinese were the first people to use the compass in the 4th century BC, which consisted of a magnetised iron needle floating in a bowl of water.

MEGA FACT
Most Victorian steamships carried sails in case of engine failure. These were also used for extra power if there were favourable winds.

GONE TO GROUND
The *Queen Elizabeth* liner was to have served out her days as a university in Hong Kong. Unfortunately she was set on fire and sank in the harbour.

First ship builders

The Ancient Egyptians were the first to build 'real ships'. They used wooden planks that were curved at both ends. The vessels, used to sail up and down the Nile and across the sea to trade with other countries, often had huge masts held in place by ropes. Square sails helped the winds push the ships along, while men at the stern used paddles to steer the ship through the water.

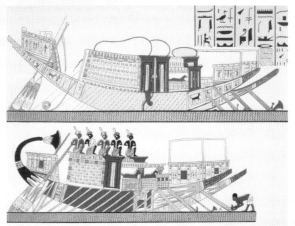

LUXURY LINER

The Normandie, below, was designed to be the biggest, fastest and most beautiful liner in the world. Launched on 29 October 1932, she was the first ship to exceed 300 metres in length. The huge, 80,000-tonne French liner had 12 decks and could carry 1,975 passengers, plus around 1,345 crew. Each of her four powerful turbo-electric engines was connected to a separate propeller shaft, giving a total of 160,000hp. With a top speed of 32.2 knots, the grand liner used 5,000 tonnes of oil per trans-atlantic crossing.

MEGA FACT
During the 1950s, the Australian government encouraged people to settle in their country. Thousands of people used passenger liners to make their journey, as they offered cheap fares.

SUPER CRUISER

Launched in 1988, the *Grand Princess* is one of the largest passenger ships in the world. Taller than the Statue of Liberty and longer than three football fields, the super liner has the capacity for 2,600 passengers.

LINERS AND CRUISE SHIPS

NORMANDIE

Built to provide 1,975 passengers with the ultimate in high-speed luxury, the *Normandie* was serviced by a crew of over 300 and nearly 1,000 domestic staff. During World War II, the US Army seized the *Normandie* and stripped out her luxurious trappings and expensive furnishings. Converted into a troopship, *Normandie* was then renamed USS *Lafayette*. The grand rooms were intended to accommodate thousands of American and foreign soldiers, but during the conversion work, a fire broke out onboard and smothered the ship in suffocating smoke.

MEGA STAR

Built in 1906, the Mauritania was the most famous Atlantic-crossing ship. Accommodating 560 first-class passengers, she had a crew of 812. The ship won the 'Blue Riband of the Atlantic' from the Kaiser Wilhelm II and held it for 22 years.

Cleveland

The Hamburg-Amerika Line's *Cleveland* was one of the first cargo liners to carry passengers and refrigerated cargo. The 17,000-tonne ship was built with accommodation for 250 first-class passengers, 392 second class, 494 third class and 2,064 emigrants. The emigrants who travelled in the crowded steerage space of most ships were kept out of view of those who paid higher fares. The *Cleveland* had a good standard of safety, but some older ships, no longer fit for use, were bought cheaply and patched up for carrying the thousands of emigrants who needed to travel. Tragically, many emigrants died during the long, gruelling journey.

Blue Riband Award

During the 19th and early 20th centuries, the passenger shipping lines of Europe and America were competing to provide the fastest, most luxurious passenger service across the North Atlantic. Competition was fierce for the coveted 'Blue Riband of the Atlantic', awarded to the liner making the fastest crossing. The *Mauritania* held the Riband from 1907 until 1929, and had a top speed of 50 km/h.

QUEEN ELIZABETH 2

The QE2 was launched in 1970 to replace the *Queen Mary* and the *Queen Elizabeth*. Although smaller than her two predecessors, she is still a huge ship at 65,000 tonnes gross. With 12 passenger decks, 750 staterooms and the capacity to carry up to 1,892 passengers, the QE2 was the first liner built to combine the tasks of a trans-atlantic passenger liner and a luxury holiday cruise ship. During the Falkland Islands conflict of 1982, the Ministry of Defence used her as a fast troopship to carry 3,000 soldiers 12,875 km non-stop to the fighting front. At a cruising speed of 28.5 knots, the QE2 made this journey faster than any other ship at the time.

MEGA FACT
The Panama Canal links the Pacific and the Atlantic Oceans so that ships do not have to go all the way around South America.

LINERS AND CRUISE SHIPS

UNITED STATES

Costing a staggering US$74 million to build in 1952, the *United States* was the largest and fastest liner ever built. Following huge publicity, the ship's inaugural voyage was sold out well in advance. Living up to her owners' expectations, the *United States* steamed the 2,942 nautical miles from Ambrose Lightship to Bishop Rock in 3 days, 10 hours and 40 minutes, at an average speed of 35.59 knots. She made the crossing back in 3 days, 12 hours and 12 minutes at an average speed of 34.51 knots – winning the 'Blue Riband' from the Queen Mary.

TITANIC

White Star Line's ship *Titanic* sailed on her fateful first voyage to New York from Queenstown, Ireland, on 11 April 1912. Onboard were 1,318 passengers and a crew of 885. Four days later, the ship struck an iceberg off the Newfoundland coast, ripping a hole in the ship's starboard side, below the waterline. In under three hours, the *Titanic* broke in half and sank. At that time, regulations stated that the number of lifeboats carried on a ship was dependent upon the tonnage of the vessel and not the number of passengers. This meant the *Titanic* had only enough lifeboats for half the people onboard, leaving 916 passengers and 673 of the crew to die in the freezing water.

Parsons' Turbine Engines

All steam engines, including turbines, are powered by high-pressure steam being allowed to expand. Before Charles Parsons' invention, patented in 1884, turbine designs had been inefficient. Parsons realised that this was because the steam was expanded in a single step. He believed that if steam was allowed to expand gradually, then higher efficiencies could be reached. Parsons' prototype had fifteen stages of expansion. The steam expanded through successive rings of moving blades on a shaft and fixed blades in a casing, producing purely rotary movement.

LUSITANIA

The *Lusitania* and her sister *Mauritania* were the first liners to use the Parsons' steam turbine. Launched on 7 June 1906, the *Lusitania* was the largest vessel afloat at the time. Marking her a pioneer in maritime history, the ship's quadruple-screw propulsion unit was driven by direct-drive steam turbines that could drive the Lusitania at 25 knots. During World War I, the ship set off on its last voyage, sailing from New York, USA, on 1 May 1941. By 7 May, with 1,959 passengers onboard, the ship had entered enemy waters. A torpedo fired by an enemy submarine hit the ship and the *Lusitania* sank, killing 1,198 people.

MEGA FACT
After the tragic sinking of the Titanic, new regulations required ships to carry sufficient lifeboats to carry everyone onboard. The wreck of the Titanic was discovered on 1 September 1985.

OCEAN LINERS AND CRUISE SHIPS

QUEEN MARY

The Queen Mary could travel at a speed of over 30 knots. The liner made its maiden voyage on 27 May 1936, on the Southampton-Cherbourg-New York route. In the first year of service, the ship had carried 56,895 passengers. After making her last commercial voyage from Southampton on 30 August 1939, the Queen Mary was converted into a World War II troopship. During its war service, the ship travelled over 960,000 km and carried nearly 800,000 people.

On 27 September 1946 the Queen Mary was handed back to Cunard, the shipping cruise line. After making her last trans-atlantic crossing on 16 September 1967, the liner was sold to the town of Long Beach, USA, where she now stands as a museum, hotel and conference centre.

SS Great Western

The Great Western Steamship Company was founded in 1836 as a sea extension of the Great Western Railway, to build a steamship to cross the Atlantic, from Bristol, England. Designed by Isambard Kingdom Brunel, the *Great Western* was launched in 1837. A wooden auxiliary paddle steamer, she was remarkable for her great strength. In 1838 the ship crossed from Bristol to New York in around 151 days. The SS *Great Western* was the first steamship constructed for trans-atlantic service and carried 148 passengers.

MEGA POWER

Ships that need to travel fast like ferries, hovercrafts and warships usually have gas turbine engines. Turbines allow a ship to go faster because of their small size and light weight. These types of engines can be up to 80 per cent lighter and 60 per cent smaller than diesel engines of the same power.

Size comparisons

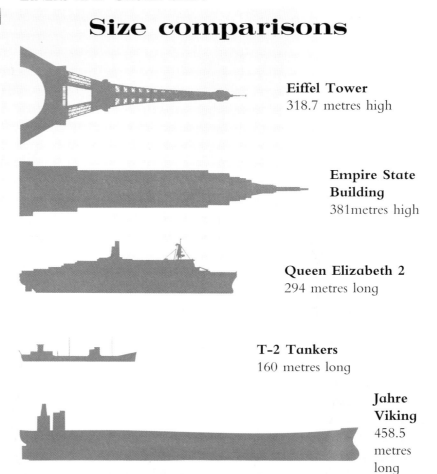

Eiffel Tower
318.7 metres high

Empire State Building
381metres high

Queen Elizabeth 2
294 metres long

T-2 Tankers
160 metres long

Jahre Viking
458.5 metres long

EXPLORER OF THE SEAS

This luxury cruise liner, with its own diesel-electric power station, was launched on 28 October 2000. The ship has a total length of 311.1 metres, a breadth of 38.6 metres and a height from the keel to the funnel top of 72.3 metres. *Explorer of the Seas* has a passenger capacity of 3,840 and a crew capacity of 1,180 – a total of 5,020 people! Among the many facilities onboard is a theatre seating up to 1,350 people, an ice-skating rink, 'street' fair, four pools, a children's adventure beach, rock-climbing wall, hospital and wedding chapel!

CARGO, CONTAINERS AND TANKERS

The world's largest ships are cargo carriers, and the largest ships of all are oil tankers. These modern ships are expensive to build, so they spend as little time as possible idling in port. However, because they use the latest computerised control and navigation systems, these vessels are able to sail with only a handful of crew.

MEGA FACT
The huge metal crates loaded onto container ships come in two standard sizes, one container exactly twice the size of the other.

FACTORY FISHING SHIPS

At one time, fishermen out in their ships had to return to land as quickly as possible, where they could clean and freeze their catch of fish. This meant that the fishermen were limited to travelling within a certain area, as they had to return while their catch was fresh. Today, large 'factory' fishing ships are able to process the fish while still at sea. This ensures that the fish remains perfectly 'fresh'.

Tugs

Ocean-going ships are so big that they are difficult to steer in enclosed waters and often have trouble sailing in and out of port. This is where tugs come in. Tugs are stubby little boats that handle so well, they can work in even the tightest spaces – alongside piers, closed-off sections of canals, rivers and locks. Tucked into a tug's hull is an incredibly powerful engine that drives a huge propeller. This provides the power to tow cargo ships and oil tankers well over a hundred times as heavy as the tug.

SELF-CONTAINED!

To make loading quicker, most freight goes onboard in large, pre-packaged metal containers. With their huge hulls and decks, many modern container ships have enough room for over 6,000 containers.

MEGA FACT
Ships that carry only one kind of cargo are called 'bulk carriers'.

MEGA FAR
A big oil tanker ships about 132 million litres of petrol – enough to drive a car 47,000 times around the Earth.

CARGO, CONTAINERS AND TANKERS

READY FOR THE RETAILERS

As the huge fishing nets are wound in, the fish are removed and conveyed to a processing deck onboard the ship. Here the fish are scaled, cleaned and filleted. They are then packed into boxes and frozen in the cold store in the hold, ready for delivery to outlets on land.

MEGA FAR
Some builders of large Japanese tankers issue their crew with bicycles to travel around the huge ships.

Torrey Canyon

Built in North America in 1959 the Torrey Canyon was the first of the big supertankers, with a cargo capacity of 60,000 tonnes. She was later expanded to twice that capacity in Japan, giving 63,000 tonnes for the ship and 120,000 for the cargo. On 18 March 1967 the oil tanker, travelling at a speed of 17 knots, struck Pollard's Rock in the Seven Stones reef between the Scilly Isles and Land's End, England, tearing open six tanks. Over the next few weeks, all the oil escaped. The oil spread along the shores of the south coast of England and the Normandy coast of France and killed most of the marine life in the region. Because no set plans had been made for a disaster of this type and size, several different emergency measures were attempted. But these only made matters worse. Chemical dispersants sprayed onto the oil slicks proved to be more lethal than the original oil.

Oil spills

Oil floats on salt water found in the sea and usually floats on fresh water (found in rivers and lakes). Oil spreads rapidly across the water surface to form a thin layer called an 'oil slick'. As the spreading continues, the layer becomes thinner, finally becoming a rainbow-coloured 'sheen'. To stop oil spreading further, attempts may be made to set fire to the oil with rockets from aircraft.

Detergent can also be sprayed on the oil to prevent it coming ashore and ruining beaches. More recent methods of dealing with such spillage include placing a boom (a type of container) around the spillage area and sinking the oil by adding ash deposits from furnaces. Oil tankers like the *Magdala* move huge cargoes of crude oil all around the world. Oil spillage in open sea therefore causes wide-spread global damage. One of the largest oil spills was caused by the *Exxon Valdez*. In 1989, the medium-sized oil tanker ran aground in the Gulf of Alaska, USA, spilling over 41 million litres of oil. The resulting slick covered more than 1,600 kilometres of the Alaska coastline and cost billions of pounds in environmental damages.

SALVAGE VESSELS

Salvage vessels are used for the underwater recovery of a ship and her contents or to assist vessels that are sinking or disabled at sea. Salvage tugs help search for wreckage and survivors when ships have sunk or aircraft have gone down over the sea. The most common causes of casualty are machinery breakdown at sea, hull damage and cargo shifting from storms. Recovery usually requires taking the ship under tow and bringing it into port.

Many salvage vessels in service today carry a magnetic detector to locate metal debris.

MEGA USEFUL
The world uses 13.5 billion litres of oil every day. We use oil to:
- make medicines, ink, fertilisers, pesticides, paints and varnishes
- fuel our cars, trucks and buses
- heat our homes
- lubricate machinery such as bicycles and printing presses
- make asphalt to pave roads
- make plastics toys, portable radios and CD players
- produce electricity

SHIPS AT WORK

From the invention of the sailing ship, it took thousands of years to build a simple steamship. Then, within a relatively short period of time, ships using nuclear and gas turbine engines and super-conducting electromagnetic thrusters appeared. Today, there are ships that can 'fly' and the technology to produce catamarans that carry cargo! In the future, ships may be able to use energy from the Sun. These will burn hydrogen in special engines and the only exhaust would be water vapour.

MEGA FACT

Inboard diesel engines are used to power all kinds of sea vessels, from yachts and fishing boats to tugs and tankers. These engines are strong, low on maintenance costs and use relatively little fuel.

THUMBS DOWN!

Although development of nuclear merchant ships began in the 1950s, it has not been commercially successful. This is due to public resistance to the general use of nuclear fuel as well as the reluctance of commercial ports to handle nuclear-powered ships like the *Otto Hahn*, fearing the possibility of radioactive leakage.

Steaming ahead

In 1790, John Fitch ran the first steamship service up the Delaware river in the USA. At that time, the easiest way to travel was by river, so many new paddle steamers were built. Flowing from Canada to the Gulf of Mexico, the Mississippi river is famous for its colourful steamboats. Powered by a large paddle wheel at the stern, these vessels first steamed out of New Orleans in 1812. Today, tourists can still travel on the world's largest riverboat, the 116-metre long *Mississippi Queen*.

NUCLEAR-POWERED COMMERCIAL SHIPS

Although the initial installation is expensive, and the shielding that must enclose a ship's reactor is large and heavy, a nuclear-powered vessel has the advantage of being able to operate for up to two years without refuelling. With the rising cost of conventional, carbon-based fuel, this could be an attractive alternative for ship builders.

MEGA FACT
Whatever their cargo, the basic tanker design is the same. Cargo is carried in insulated tanks, or compartments, within the main tank that forms the largest part of the hull.

OTTO HAHN

OTTO HAHN

Commissioned in 1962, the US military built the nuclear-powered ship NS *Savannah*. Although the vessel was a technical success, it was not economically viable and was decommissioned (put out of use) eight years later. The German-built *Otto Hahn* cargo ship and research facility sailed some 650,000 nautical miles on 126 voyages in 10 years without any technical problems. This ship also proved too expensive to operate and was later converted to diesel.

CABLE INNOVATOR CABLE LAYER

The *Cable Innovator* is the world's largest vessel of its kind, specifically designed for fibre-optic cable laying. Built by Kvaerner Masa of Finland, the vessel can operate in extreme weather and is equipped to use a remotely operated vehicle (ROV). The *Cable Innovator* has a conventional cable instrumentation system plus two computerised systems. It is powered by five Wartsila Vasa diesel engines, which provide a total power of 12.8MW. The ship has no rudder, but there are two tunnel thrusters located at the stern.

STANISLAV YUDIN

This Ice class III A2 crane vessel flies under the Russian Flag. Built in 1985, the *Stanislav Yudin* was upgraded in 1993 and 1996. With a maximum transit speed of 12 knots, the ship has been employed for platform installations and removals, salvage and installation of large sub-sea structures and in-shore lifting. With an overall length of 183.2 metres, the Stanislav Yudin can accommodate 135 people. It has its own helicopter deck and is equipped with an active computerised lifting analysing system, also suitable for simulation of load conditions. The vessel is offered for use in the North Sea, West Africa, Mediterranean, Middle East and Gulf of Mexico.

MEGA TIME-WARP!

Japanese shipyard Nippon Kokan experimented by fitting computer-controlled square sails to a small tanker, for setting when the wind was favourable. A saving of 10 per cent in fuel costs was achieved in just one year!

WIG CRAFT

The first serious WIG ('wing-in-ground' effect) boats were developed in the 1960s. The FlareCraft is one of a new kind of WIG craft that combines the speed of an aeroplane with the characteristics of a boat. A 225-hp engine provides power for 'flight' and propels the vessel to speeds in excess 160 km/h. But the FlareCraft cannot fly higher than 2 metres above the waves, which is why it is registered as a sea vessel. Other ship companies are developing similar WIG vessels, capable of carrying cargo and passengers.

JAHRE VIKING

The world's biggest tanker operating today is the *Jahre Viking*. Formerly known as *Happy Giant* and *Seawise Giant*, the already enormous vessel was converted in 1980 from another tanker by the insertion of an additional mid-ship section. This increased the overall length of the ship to 458.5 metres. Now measuring 260,851 gross register tonnes, *Jahre Viking* has a dead-weight tonnage (cargo capacity) of 564,763 tonnes.

Ice-breaking power

Nuclear propulsion of ships was born out of the research into the atomic bombs that were dropped on Japan at the end of World War II. Although the use of nuclear power for commercial ships has proved unsuccessful in other countries, the Russians have used nuclear propulsion for their giant ice-breakers. The first of these huge vessels was the *Lenin*. Commissioned in 1959 the ship, which had three nuclear reactors as her power plant, remained in service for 30 years. Although extremely expensive to run, the *Lenin*'s cost was justified as her massive power was needed to punch a way through the ice in order to keep open the northern sea route stretching from Novaya Semla to the Bering Sea.

BOTNICA MULTI-PURPOSE ICE-BREAKER

The *Botnica*, a combined ice-breaker, tug and supply vessel, is one of the most advanced vessels of her type. Built in Finland, she was delivered in 1998 to the Finnish Maritime Administration (FMA). *Botnica* is run on a diesel-electric plant. Six packages of twin Caterpillar 3512B units connected to six ABB generators power a thruster system of two 5MW Azipods. The thrusters can be used to make a propeller wave that pushes broken ice away from the hull, leaving a wider channel for commercial merchant vessels to follow.

MEGA FACT
Most ships today are fitted with radar. This shows the captain if there is another ship nearby so the ship can turn away to avoid a collision.

MOTORCYCLES

In little over a hundred years, the motorcycle has progressed from the first boneshakers, which were little more than bicycles, to the high-tech, fast and furious vehicles on the road today.

BIKE BASICS

From nipping down to the shops to touring the countryside or speeding on a racing circuit, there are different motorcycles for every kind of driver. In this chapter, you'll find bikes ranging from the earliest wooden and brass models, to the most powerful designs of today. Check out some of the wacky 'oddballs' that have appeared over the years – or drool over the most expensive motorcycles imaginable! First, let's look at the basics.

Storage compartment

The four main sections of a motorcycle are: the frame, the engine (with gearbox and drive components), the wheels and the petrol tank.

Passenger back rest

Motorcycles (like this Harley-Davidson tourer) have wire-spoked wheels, whereas scooters usually have solid wheels like those of a car.

Exhaust

MEGA MILEAGE

Depending on the size of the engine, a motorcycle may run up to 36 km per litre — about four times that of most mid-sized cars.

SAFETY FIRST

There's no doubt about it — motorcycles can be dangerous if they're not used correctly. Training is a must: steering, accelerating and braking require skill and a high degree of coordination. The proper outfit is essential too. In addition to the helmet (which is vital) motorcyclists need to wear as much leather clothing as possible to protect them should they fall. This includes gloves, boots, jackets and chaps or full-body riding suits.

The term 'cc' refers to the cylinder capacity of a vehicle. The bigger the cc — the more power you get! Cylinder capacity of a motorcycle can range from 250 to 1500 or even higher.

The front wheel and axle are attached to the frame with a 'fork', a two-pronged pivoting arm.

Disc brake

Handlebar control for the engine

Petrol tank

Two-stroke and four-stroke engines are used for motorcycles. The power is transmitted to the rear wheel through the gearbox and then through sprockets and chains, or through a drive shaft.

BONESHAKERS

Motorcycles have been around for over 100 years but it's difficult to recognise the very first models as the same sleek, powerful machines we know today. They originally descended from push bikes, and most of the first motorcycles were little more than ordinary bicycles with a simple motor attached which drove the back wheel. Some of these 'boneshakers' even had pedals – so the rider could help the motor!

MEGA FACT
The first motorised bicycle, the Michaux-Perraux, was built in 1868. It reached a top speed of 30 km/h on its first run.

A BUMPY RIDE
Early models were called 'boneshakers' for good reason. Lack of suspension, plus the bumpy country roads of the day, meant cyclists were in for a shaky ride!

The First Motorcycle

It was German engineer Gottlieb Daimler (who later formed the Daimler-Benz company with Karl Benz) who earned the nickname 'Father of the Motorcycle'.

In 1885, Daimler built the first motorcycle that used petrol. It was constructed mostly of wood, with wooden-spoked, iron-banded wagon wheels. But the vehicle also had two smaller wheels at either side, and technically this disqualified it as a true bicycle. Yet most historians consider this model to be the first motorcycle. Daimler's son, Paul, was the first to ride his father's invention, for nearly 10 km – until the engine became so hot it set the saddle on fire!

PART EXCHANGE

Regular bicycle wheels soon became too weak for motorcycles, and sturdier designs were constructed to take their place. Pedals disappeared altogether as more powerful engines came on the market.

A PLACE IN HISTORY

The motorcycle was the world's first form of personal mechanised transport, pre-dating the car by 25 years. Designers of early motorcycles took a long time deciding where to put the engine. One memorable model even towed its engine in a trailer!

MEGA FACT

In 1881, a steam tricycle was exhibited at the Stanley Bicycle Show in London. Despite attracting many orders, British law made it illegal for such self-powered vehicles to be used on public roads at the time!

THE CLASSICS

For almost a century now, the name Harley-Davidson has been synonymous with motorcycles. Since the company began production with the 'Silent Gray Fellow' in 1904, Harley-Davidson hasn't looked back. But other manufacturers of the day, such as Triumph, Indian and Honda, have given us a few well-loved classics to remember too...

ALL-TIME CLASSIC

When it comes to motorcycles, the 1936 Harley-Davidson 61E wins the vote for the classic of all-time! A highly technical model, it set the design for all Harleys that followed. With its rounded tank, stylish instrument console and curving mudguards, the 61E quickly took the lead in American motorcycle design.

PUSH-ME-PULL-YOU

The front and back wheels of the Harley-Davidson 61E were interchangeable, which was a common feature of motorcycles during the 1930s.

Big Harleys are nicknamed 'Hogs' because of their great size.

MEGA CLASSIC
When Harley-Davidson was first incorporated in 1907, the company made only 150 motorcycles in a year. By 1909 production had increased to eight times that amount.

Harley-Davidson Milestones

1901 Harley-Davidson founders begin design experiments.

1907 The Harley-Davidson company is incorporated.

1909 Trademark 45 degree V-Twin engine is introduced.

1916–18 Harleys called to duty in World War I.

1920 H-D becomes the world's largest motorcycle manufacturer.

1936 The H-D Knucklehead is introduced.

1939–44 Harleys called to duty in World War II.

1965 Land speed record is set on a modified Harley Sprint.

1976-8 Harleys win the AMA Championship three years running.

THE 'KNUCKLEHEAD'

The 61E earned this name as the engine resembled a clenched fist. The rocker covers form the 'knuckles'!

EASY RIDERS

Not all motorcyclists like riding super fast – many like to sit back and cruise along the open road. These bikers are called 'Easy Riders'. To them, style and comfort are more important than speed. Harleys are the world's most popular bikes with Easy Riders.

MEGA DUTY

In 1907 Harley-Davidsons were being sold for police duty for the first time. Harleys were also used later by the military in both World Wars.

BMW R1200 C

In one of the most dramatic chase scenes ever seen on film, James Bond skilfully rides a BMW R1200 over the rooftops in the 1997 movie, *Tomorrow Never Dies*. It was one of very few motorcycles ever to be used in a James Bond film, and it's not difficult to see why the movie-makers chose this particular model. The R1200 was BMW's first ever cruiser, launched in 1997, but with its high US-style handlebars and impressive five-speed gearbox, it's already becoming a truly modern classic.

TRIUMPH X75 HURRICANE

Britain's Craig Vetter was commissioned by BSA-Triumph to style a limited production version of their three-cylinder motorcycle for the US market. One of the most striking modifications was the three-pipe exhaust system and extended forks. With its 740cc engine, four-speed gearbox and a top speed of 170 km/h, the Triumph Hurricane is a firm favourite with collectors.

MEGA FACT
Fewer than 1200 Hurricanes had been built when Triumph closed its factory in 1974. Despite this, the model made its mark and greatly influenced motorcycle design that followed.

INDIAN CHIEF

The Indian Chief dominated the motorcycle market for an incredible twenty years! But by the 1950s, the bike was outdated compared to its adversary, the Harley Knucklehead. Nearly 12,000 Chiefs were built in a choice of black, red, blue and white. Reaching a top speed of 137 km/h, they weren't exactly the fastest bikes around, but with their smooth, classic looks – who cared!

HONDA GOLD WING ASPENCADE 1100cc SE

Launched in 1975, the original Honda GL™1000 Gold Wing was Japan's biggest, most complex bike ever produced. With a performance that matched anything on the market, the Gold Wing revolutionised motorcycle design. Then, in 1984, the Gold Wing Aspencade was introduced. A new 1100cc engine and high-performance chassis were the basis of this luxury tourer. The hydraulic valve adjuster system provided quicker starts, faster warm-ups – and quieter running.

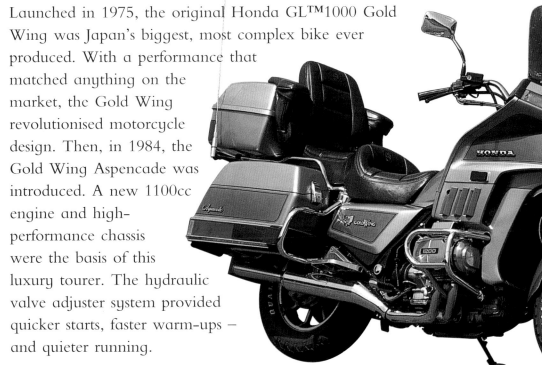

ARIEL SQUARE FOUR

Production of the Ariel Square Four began in England in 1930. The design used two crankshafts geared together with the two vertical twin-cylinders arranged in a square formation (hence its name). In 1949, the engine was redesigned with a light alloy block and head to form the Mark I. The Square Four Mark II came along in 1953, featuring detachable light alloy exhaust manifolds on each side.

MEGA CLASSIC
Fewer than 4,000 Ariel MkIIs were built, and production ended in 1959. The bike was proclaimed by many to be the world's most exclusive motorcycle.

NORTON COMMANDO

The first Norton Commando motorcycle can be traced back to the late 1940s, when the Model 7 Twin was launched. This evolved into the 650cc Dominator and 750cc Atlas, before being launched as the 750cc Commando in 1967. During its 10 years in production, the Commando was very popular. In a pole conducted in the UK it was voted 'Machine of the Year' for five successive years (1968-1972). Enhanced by its light weight and slim profile, the 1969 chassis featured special engine mountings which helped to reduce vibration.

BROUGH SUPERIOR SS100

The Rolls-Royce of motorcycles, Brough-Superior is surely the most distinguished marque in motorcycle history. Powerful and expensive, the SS100s were introduced in 1925 and are now one of the most sought-after of all collectors' bikes, not least because of their connection with English soldier and author, T.E. Lawrence (Lawrence of Arabia). Brough achieved many racing successes and speed records – in 1938 one bike reached 290 km/h in Budapest. Unfortunately the rider, Eric Fernihough, crashed and was killed on the return run, and his record was never officially recorded.

MEGA FACT
Lawrence of Arabia (1888-1935) was an enthusiastic motorcyclist and owned many Brough motorcycles!

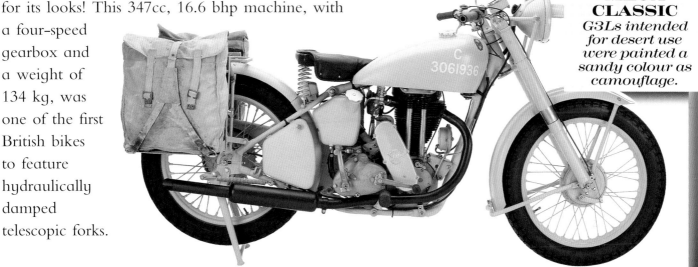

MATCHLESS G3L

Founded in 1899, Matchless was one of the first British motorcycle manufacturers. The 1941 G3L was a typical single-cylinder machine. Over 80,000 were built just for the British forces during World War II. Okay, so they're not the most elegant of machines, but the G3L was built for its sturdiness, reliability and endurance – not for its looks! This 347cc, 16.6 bhp machine, with a four-speed gearbox and a weight of 134 kg, was one of the first British bikes to feature hydraulically damped telescopic forks.

MEGA CLASSIC
G3Ls intended for desert use were painted a sandy colour as camouflage.

THE MONSTERS

Introducing the most powerful motorcycles ever made – the top speed of a Harley VR1000 is off the speedometer of most cars, let alone most motorcycles! Read on to find out more about these monster road bikes.

A TOP MONSTER

This Harley-Davidson VR1000 is a prime example of a powerful 'monster' bike. Its amazing engine has a pulling-power equal to the joint efforts of no less than 135 horses!

MEGA FACT
Because of its power and manoeuvrability, US police are once again choosing the traditional Harley to patrol many city streets.

MEGA FACT
Most motorcycles have manual gearboxes. Only a few companies, like Honda and Moto Guzzi, have designed semi- and automatic models.

Monster Bike Must-Haves

Mega powerful models have these common features:

- **A big muffler** to reduce the noise of the powerful engine
- A curved windshield, forcing the air smoothly over and around the motorcycle
- **Tapered styling** at the back to reduce wind-drag, therefore increasing speed
- High-performance tyres to give stability at top speeds

FAST AND FURIOUS!

Japanese bikes may take the lead in many motorcycle sports today, but US Harleys are still tops on the dirt track.

MEGA FACT

In 1970, Harley rider Cal Rayborn reached an amazing speed of 427 km/h on his cigar-shaped bike at the Salt Lake Flats in Utah, USA.

SUZUKI BANDIT

Top Japanese manufacturers Suzuki have a long history of producing high-performance machines like the Bandit. In 2000, this model received a complete makeover, giving it the agility of a middleweight sport bike and a top speed of 206 km/h. This only improved upon the award-winning performance and style which have already made the Bandit a cult classic.

TRIUMPH T509 SPEED TRIPLE

Tom Cruise made this striking motorcycle famous in his 2000 film, *Mission Impossible II*. Its stunning hi-tech appearance, combined with the awesome performance of a superbike, provided the attitude that's perfect for an action movie. Thanks to its extreme popularity, the Speed Triple has helped re-establish Triumph as one of the top marques in the industry.

MEGA FAST
The world's first eight-cylinder motorcycle was built by an American aviator and engine producer, Glenn Curtiss.

MEGA FACT
Trailbreakers have hollow aluminium wheels which hold 17 litres of fuel. With the wheels empty, these bikes can even float in water!

ROKON TRAILBREAKER

The Rokon Trailbreaker was designed to go anywhere! This all-terrain motorcycle can climb steep mountain slopes, plough through the deepest mud, or haul heavy loads. It's popular with firefighters, farmers, mountaineers and hunters.

Trailbreakers have even been used by Brazilian Marines, who found the vehicles more capable in muddy terrain than some of their own tracked army vehicles.

ULTRA AVENGER

Ultra cycles are custom-built bikes which are designed to suit each individual rider. Choosing from hundreds of options means you can create the bike of your dreams. It comes at a price though – US$25,000 for this 1999 Ultra Avenger!

MEGA FACT
The most popular era for motorcycles to date was the late 1960s, when British makers alone built 70,000 bikes per year.

AMAZING BUT TRUE

EVEL KNIEVEL

Born on 17 October 1938, in Montana, USA, Robert Craig Knievel – or Evel Knievel as he became better known – is probably the most famous motorcycle stunt rider of all time!

An outstanding skier and ice hockey player, he began his daredevil career in 1965. Forming a troupe called Evel Knievel's Motorcycle Daredevils, he regularly rode through fire walls and was towed at 320 km/h behind dragster race cars while holding on to a parachute!

In 1966, Evel decided to start touring alone. On 1 January 1968, he jumped 45 metres across the fountains in front of Caesar's Palace in Las Vegas, USA. Although he cleared the fountains, his landing was a complete disaster, and his injuries left him in a coma for 30 days. The injuries didn't stop him though, and Evel continued performing his daredevil stunts around the world until his retirement in 1976.

MEGA MONEY

For a jump over the Snake River Canyon in Idaho, USA, legendary daredevil Evel Knieval was paid a staggering US$6,000,000!

Evel's Memorable Moments:

1968   On New Year's Day ...shed while trying to jump the ... at Caesar Palace in Las Vegas,

1970   Successfully cleared 13 cars in Seattle, USA, on 9 September.

1971   Set a world record in Ontario, Canada, by jumping 19 Dodge cars.

1974   Successfully jumped 40.5 metres over three trucks at the Canadian National Exposition on 20 August.

1975   Over 90,000 spectators at Wembley Stadium, London, watched as Evel crashed upon landing, breaking his pelvis after clearing 13 double-decker buses.

1976   Evel suffered a concussion and two broken arms during an attempt to jump a tank full of live sharks in Chicago, USA. For the first time a bystander was also injured, eventually losing an eye. Evel decided to retire from major performances.

🎯 Record-Breakers 🎯

The world's tallest rideable motorcycle (left) was built by Tom Wiberg of Sweden. This record-breaking vehicle measures an amazing 2.3 metres high and 4.7 metres long!

The fastest time for a run over 400 metres is 6.19 seconds, held by American Tony Lang (above), who rode a supercharged Suzuki in Gainesville, Florida, USA, in 1994.

In 1996 Douglas and Roger Bell, from Western Australia, designed and built a bike (above) with a record length of 7.6 metres.

The Harley-Davidson Owners Group (HOG) is the world's largest company-sponsored motorcycle enthusiasts' group – with over 400,000 members in more than 1000 branches world-wide.

The world's most expensive production motorcycle is the Morbidelli 850 V8 (left), which in 1998 sold for a whopping US$98,400!

ODDBALLS

These are the machines that make heads turn! They may not be the sleekest or fastest vehicles ever built, but these motorcycles and scooters are certainly among the most interesting. Let's start with a look at the super long Bohmerland!

THREE'S A CROWD!

This 1928 Bohmerland from the Czech Republic was an extra-long motorcycle that seated three people. Many features combined to make this bike a real oddball. Apart from its great length, it had two fuel tanks which were mounted on each side of the rear wheel (rather than under the engine as usual) and the frame was made of tubular steel.

Unfortunately, the Bohmerland was not produced in great numbers due to the start of World War II in 1939.

The Ultimate Caddy

The Bobcat was the ultimate caddy, enabling golfers to speed round the course in record time. This two-wheeled linkster had a clever self-standing centre stand, which was activated when the golfer's weight left the seat. Although the cart is no longer in production, the Chicago-based manufacturer is still in business, building Bobcat skip loaders.

The Bohmerland's 16-horsepower four-stroke engine delivered a top speed of 95 km/h.

A racing version of the Czech Bohmerland, which had a shorter wheel base, did exist once. But it's this super long road version which has become a classic oddball.

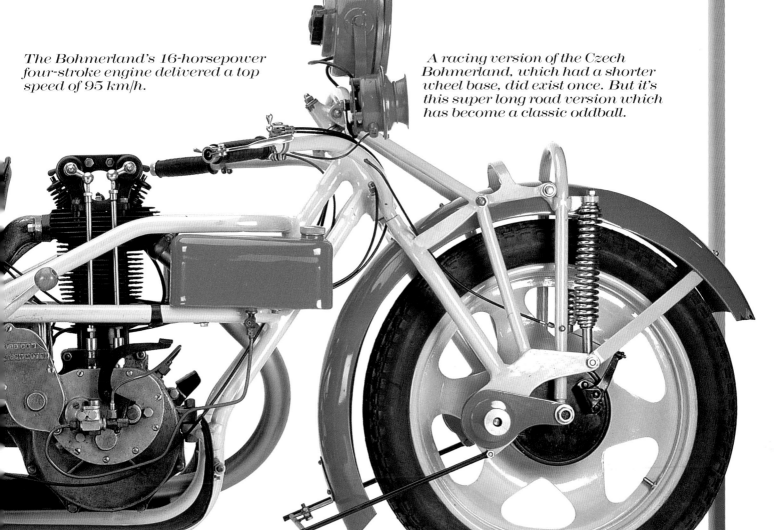

The Bohmerland was the first motorcycle to feature solid wheels cast from light alloy. Such wheels are now common on motorcycles.

ODDBALLS

AUTOPED

The Autoped was little more than a motorised version of a child's scooter. Made in New York City in 1917, this model was an instant success as it allowed riders to weave in and out of the confused mixture of trolleys, horses and cars that crowded the city's streets at the time.

The Autoped's steering column could be folded down for easy storage.

The seatless Autoped was designed to be driven standing up!

THE WILLIAMS

Although it never went into full production, the 1917 Williams is one of the most unusual motorcycles ever made. Note the footboards – they're also a mechanism which the rider pumps to start the engine. The 3-cylinder engine was built into the rear of the machine, and it would spin with the rear wheel.

CUSHMAN MODEL 52

After World War II, the Cushman company took advantage of the scooter boom in the USA and manufactured a range of models, including the 52 (below). This stylish scooter boasted a 4-horsepower engine delivering a top speed of 65 km/h. The Model 52 was nicknamed the 'Turtleback'. Can you see why?

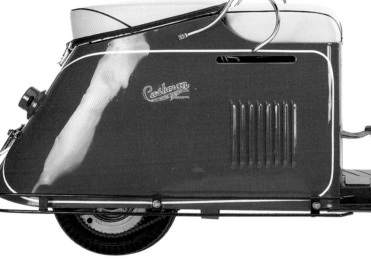

MEGA FACT
Scooters have become fashionable again with the help of recent cool models like the plastic-bodied Yamaha BW12.

NER-A-CAR

The 1923 'Nearly-A-Car' was truly an oddball! The maker's choice of name was meant to convince customers that the machine combined the best qualities of both a car and a motorcycle. It was more enclosed than most motorcycles, with lots of mudguarding to prevent the rider's clothes from getting dirty. Its low centre of gravity also made for easier handling.

MEGA FACT
The Ner-A-Car is said to have been especially popular with vicars because the open frame enabled them to ride wearing their cassocks!

CARS

When cars first appeared in the early 1900s, no one could have imagined the impact they would have on everyday life. The latest cars on the roads little resemble the early models like Ford's famous Tin Lizzy.

THE CAR CLOSE-UP

Since they were invented in the late 1800s, cars have developed at an incredible rate. Some models are not only a means of transportation, they're practically works of art! On the following pages you'll discover the fastest, the strangest, the most amazing cars of all time. Read about the history of the car and why some become classics. See the cars your parents might have driven in the 1970s – and what you might be driving in future! But first, how do these things work?

MEGA CRAWL
There are millions of cars in the world today, so it's no surprise that the roads are over-crowded. In some large cities, the average speed of traffic is the same as it was when we used horse-drawn carriages to get around!

Power steering makes manoeuvring easier when driving slowly or turning in small spaces.

POWER SOURCES

Before engines were invented, nature was the only source of power available. Animals pulled carts, and the earliest machines used wind or water power. Then came the steam engine, followed by the internal combustion engine in 1860, which revolutionised our lives. Most cars today use a four-stroke combustion cycle, known as the four-cycle engine, to convert petrol into motion.

There are two types of hydraulic brake systems used on cars — drum and disc. Most cars, like this 1992 Porsche Carrera, have discs at the front and drums at the rear.

How a four-cycle engine works

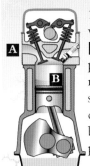

1. The intake valve opens **A** and the piston **B** moves down so the engine can take in both air and petrol.

2. Then the piston moves back up and the mixture is squashed. This is called 'compression'.

3. A spark from a spark plug **C** makes this mixture explode. This is called 'combustion'.

4. The explosion pushes the piston down and waste gases escape through the exhaust valve **D**.

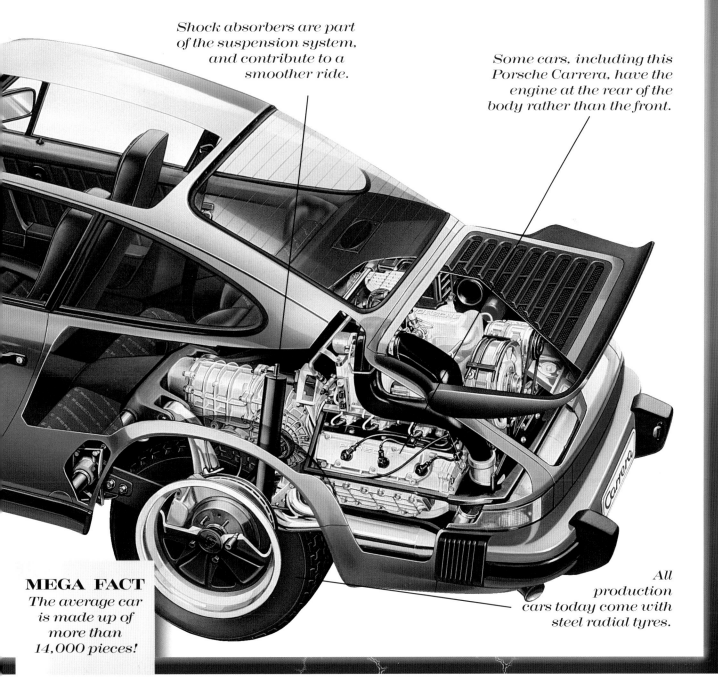

Shock absorbers are part of the suspension system, and contribute to a smoother ride.

Some cars, including this Porsche Carrera, have the engine at the rear of the body rather than the front.

MEGA FACT
The average car is made up of more than 14,000 pieces!

All production cars today come with steel radial tyres.

FIRST ON FOUR WHEELS

The first car-like vehicle, the horseless carriage, was designed by Karl Benz and was on the road as early as 1886. Other budding designers soon followed his lead, including Henry Ford with his famous Model T (shown below). With the rapid advancement of the combustion engine, it was only a matter of time before Ford's dream became reality – and motor cars were everywhere!

TIN LIZZY INTERNATIONAL

The first Model T Ford was assembled near Detroit, Michigan, USA. But although Detroit produced the majority of Model Ts (or 'Tin Lizzies' as they became known), many were built in other countries such as Canada and England.

"YOU CAN PAINT IT ANY COLOUR... AS LONG AS IT'S BLACK!"

Although there is no proof that Henry Ford actually spoke these words, the phrase has always been linked with his name, and has survived for almost a century.

MODEL T MILLIONS

Between 1908 and 1927, Ford built a staggering 15 million cars with the Model T engine. Apart from the modern-day Volkswagen Beetle, this is the longest run of any single model in history!

The Life of Henry Ford

BORN 30 July 1863, Greenfield Township, Michigan, USA.

c. 1879 Leaves the family farm for Detroit to work in machine shops.

1899 Ends eight years of employment with the Edison Illuminating Co. to devote full attention to the manufacture of automobiles.

1903 Ford Motor Co. is officially incorporated.

1908 Begins manufacturing the famous Model T.

c. 1913-4 Introduces the first moving automobile assembly line.

1947 Dies 7 April at Fair Lane, his estate in Michigan.

ELECTRIC EXPERIMENTS

Long before the engine-driven car arrived, experiments with electric cars operated by battery power were underway. Although these models (dating from as early as 1834) successfully reached the production stage, they never quite caught on with the public.

TOP DOGS

Other top names in the industry's early years included Benz, Austin, Fiat, Renault and General Motors (home of Cadillac and Chrysler).

MODEL T FORD

Over the years, a wide variety of bodies were available, including vans, closed cars and even truck versions. Special bodies and many other parts could be bought easily, so it was possible to convert a Model T car to anything from a taxi to a tractor! At first, Model Ts had oil lamps and needed to be hand cranked to start the engine, which was pretty hard work!

CADILLAC MODEL 30

Cadillac made news headlines in 1908 with the announcement that it was replacing all of its lines with the Model 30. Available as a roadster, convertible, and four- and five-passenger touring cars, sales of this attractive new line were tremendous, overtaking all Cadillac sales records. The 1912 Model 30, shown here, was revolutionary – it was the first production car to offer the electric starting and ignition systems that are the foundation of what we use today.

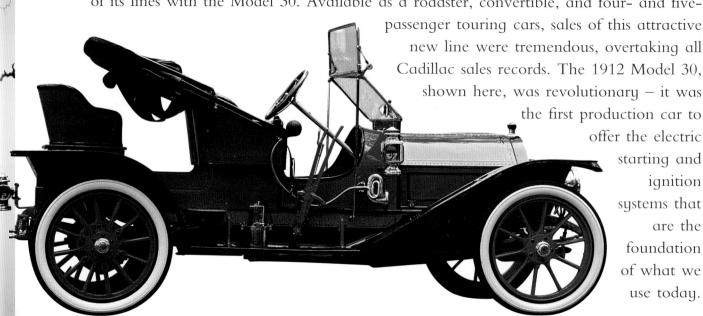

CADILLAC V-63

In 1924, Cadillac introduced a new design with a V8 engine – its most powerful motor to date. Known as the V-63, Cadillac's latest creation was a luxurious five-passenger coupé. Over 19,000 were built and Cadillac retained its reputation as 'the standard of the world'. Back then, a well-used Model T Ford could be bought for just US$20, while a new Cadillac (depending on the model) fetched up to US$5000!

BMW DIXI

The Bayerisch Motoren Werke (Bavarian Motor Company) formed in 1916 with the merger of an aircraft maker and a manufacturer of aircraft engines. After World War I, though, the Versailles Treaty would not allow German companies to produce aircraft, so BMW turned their skills to the growing motorcycle market. Naturally, the next step was the motor car. In 1928 the company bought a factory that was producing a version of the Engish Austin Seven. This economy car became BMW's first automobile – Model 3/15, affectionately known as the 'Dixi'.

THE CLASSICS

Many classic cars today are worth more than they were when new, because they are much more difficult to find. The models shown here and on the following pages are just a few of the much-loved classics from days gone by. Each model has something special about it that makes people stop and say, "Now there goes a classic!"

HERE COME THE FINS...

After World War II, the American people were hungry for new and creative designs. As part of Cadillac's war involvement, a handful of executives were exposed to top-secret government projects. At one such viewing, a Cadillac designer spotted the Lockheed Lightning P-38 fighter plane, and was inspired by its vertical 'tailfins'. The first auto fins, although quite small, appeared on the 1948 Cadillac. The public loved them, and in the years that followed they continued to grow. By the mid 1950s, all the car manufacturers were developing their own versions – trying to 'out-fin' each other!

NO KEYS? NO PROBLEM!

A few classics, like the first E-type Jaguar produced in Britain in 1961, didn't require a key to start the engine. You could simply press a button and go!

HOW MUCH MIGHT MY CLASSIC COST TODAY?

 Volkswagen Beetle (1957) £2500-7000

 Cadillac Sedan De Ville (1956) £2800-8000

 Austin-Healey Sprite (1958) £2800-8400

 Rolls Royce Silver Spirit MkI (1989) £13,400-24,500

 Chevrolet Corvette Roadster (1962) £14,000-31,500

 E-Type Jaguar XKE (1963) £12,500-38,500

 Mercedes-Benz 300SL (1954) £48,950-154,000

Note: Figures are estimates only and will vary depending on condition and region.

UP TO: £10,000   £20,000   £30,000   £40,000   £50,000 and more!

'THE BEST CAR IN THE WORLD'

Rolls Royce's classic Camargue (1975-86) earned this title because of its fine quality. Its ghostly quietness and shiny body also earned it the nickname 'Silver Ghost'.

BIG CAR, BIG TANK

Heavy duty petrol-guzzlers like the 1956 Cadillac Sedan de Ville, shown above, consumed petrol at a staggering rate of around 30 litres per 100 km!

THE CLASSICS

CADILLAC SEDAN DE VILLE

The mid 1950s and '60s will be remembered for some of the biggest, boldest cars ever, particularly in the USA. As fast as one company produced a flashy new model, a rival quickly brought out an even more outrageous one. Despite many contenders during this era, Cadillac remained the USA's luxury sales leader. Others happily sold 40,000 cars a year – that was an average quarterly output for Cadillac!

MEGA DATE
In 1956 Cadillac introduced their first hardtop Sedan de Ville (shown right).

ROLLS ROYCE SILVER SPIRIT

Britain's Rolls Royce made their first car in 1906 and they're still going strong, supplying top-quality cars for customers worldwide. One of the most luxurious models was the Silver Spirit Mark I, produced in 1980–89. The interior was dominated by a traditional wooden dash-board, with a choice of fine leather or velour upholstery.

A SMOOTH RIDE
In the 1930s, students at the Rolls Royce school for chauffeurs had to drive with a glass of water balanced on the radiator – without spilling it.

MERCEDES-BENZ 300SL 'GULLWING'

This high-performance car remains one of the most desirable models of all time! The 1954 300SL has a huge 3.0 litre fuel-injected engine capable of reaching a top speed of 224 km/h. As with many sports cars of the 1950s, there was little difference between road and racing versions. The most distinctive feature of the 300SL was the 'Gullwing' doors. When open, these upswinging doors looked just like a seagull's wings! They were vital because of the car's high seals – normal doors would have been impossible to open! Production of the 'Gullwing' ended in 1957 – in total, only 1,400 models had been built.

THE CLASSICS

AUSTIN-HEALEY SPRITE

Austin-Healey introduced the Sprite in Britain in 1958. This small and zippy sports car quickly became popular, especially with younger drivers. Because of the unusual position of the headlights high up on the body, the first version of this model was nicknamed 'Frog-Eyed Sprite'. The Mark II edition was launched in 1962, this time with the headlights in a more conventional position.

OLF 852E

E-TYPE JAGUAR

Unlike other supercars of its time, the E-type, or XKE, was produced for the mass-market and over 70,000 were built. Launched in 1961, following the success of the C- and D-types, this popular British sports car with a 3.8 litre 6-cylinder engine could reach speeds of almost 240 km/h. In 1969, the series 11 E-types boasted several revisions, including a collapsible steering column – and the famous Jaguar starter button on the dashboard was replaced by the standard key start.

CHEVROLET CORVETTE

The Chevy Corvette first appeared in 1953 as an American entry into the sports car market, which at one time was dominated by European makes. The second generation Corvette, with its fuel-injection engine, was launched in 1963. This model even had a racing version, the Z-06. Luxury options such as power steering, air conditioning and leather seats were also available for the first time on these models. By 1968 the Corvette had changed dramatically in appearance and now had hidden windshield wipers and removable T-tops on coupé models.

VOLKSWAGEN BEETLE

Production of the classic VW Beetle began in 1940, but the factory was forced to close in 1944 due to World War II. After the war production resumed, but as materials were in short supply these early models were very primitive. (The interiors were stuck together with a fish-based glue, which gave off a dreadful smell!) In the 1960s the Beetle became most popular, and even gained cult status, when hippies considered it a symbol of peace.

MEGA FACT
The Volkswagen Beetle, with sales exceeding 20 million since the 1940s, holds the record for history's longest production run.

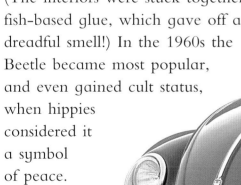

AAAHH...
When the VW Beetle was first manufactured, many people said it wouldn't sell — they thought it was too ugly!

POWER TRIP

Muscle cars and monster trucks are made to be big, powerful, reliable and most of all, exciting! Introduced in the 1960s, the first muscle cars were fast, 'tyre-smoking', relatively cheap – and designed to be noticed. With no thought for their heavy fuel consumption, these 'power cars' left others eating their dust. Then, in the 1970s, a number of American enthusiasts decided to 'muscle-up' their pick-up trucks, and so the monster truck was born.

Most muscle cars have a V6 or a massive V8 engine – like this one from a Chevy 502

MEGA MUSCLE
The world's fastest muscle car is the 1966 Cobra. But with a top speed of only 190 km/h, it's no match for the McLaren F1!

FORD MUSTANG

The Ford Mustang began life in 1964, and quickly topped the sales charts. More than 100,000 were sold during its first four months on the market, making it Ford's most successful car since the Model T. Considered one of the first 'muscle' cars, the Mustang quickly caught the attention of the young, who rushed out in droves to buy one. Its popular features included excellent handling, a powerful engine and a flash, distinctive design. More than 30 years after the first model went on show, new Mustangs are still selling. But the original will always be a hard act to follow!

What is... FOUR-WHEEL DRIVE?

When all four wheels of a car are powered by the engine, it's called a four-wheel drive vehicle. If one wheel gets stuck, the others still function. Four-wheel drives are as reliable in mud or snow as they are on paved road. Historians are unsure who invented the system, but the first 4WD vehicle was designed in 1900 by Ferdinand Porsche (yes, the founder of Porsche cars) for an Austrian truck manufacturer. The vehicle had electric hub motors on each wheel – powered by a generator. NASA, the American space agency, used the idea of electric wheel hub motors to put its lunar vehicle in motion!

PLYMOUTH ROADRUNNER

In 1968, Plymouth decided that muscle cars had strayed too far from their original purpose, which was to be cheap, fast and exciting. So, they paid US$50,000 to Warner Bros to affix a cartoon bird onto a new vehicle, based on a Belvedere pillared coupé. With an ultimate speed of 154 km/h, the Road Runner was born. Although it had numerous features, including beefed-up suspension and manual transmission, the interior was very basic. A horn that went 'beep-beep' was the finishing touch!

BIGFOOT

Bigfoot 1 was the first monster truck ever built, and is probably the most famous truck in the world. Starting life as a 1974 Ford F250 pick-up, Bigfoot was modified by its owner, who added bigger tyres and better suspension. Rear steering was included later. In 1981, Bigfoot began its 'car-crushing' career, performing in an American stadium. Various imitators followed, and car-crushing became a major event. By 1987 the latest-technology monster trucks were so fast, that they went from crushing other vehicles to racing them.

SPEED DEMONS

At the top of the motorcar pyramid sits the ultimate superstar – the exotic sports car. Amazingly fast and outrageously expensive, exotic production models don't need to be practical or cost-effective. With precision tuned, high-performance engines, these speed demons showcase the most advanced technologies a manufacturer has to offer.

WEIGHT CONSCIOUS

During the design of the McLaren F1, performance was the top priority, and the goal weight was set at 1,000 kg. The final weight was 1,140 kg – still 40 per cent lighter than a Lamborghini Diablo!

MCLAREN F40?

When Gordon Murray designed the McLaren F1, he had a Ferrari F40 in the workshop to study its steering system as he considered the F40 to be the world's best handling car!

Ten of the FASTEST!

Model:	Approx. Maximum Speed:		0-97 km/h (60 mph):
McLaren F1	372 km/h	(231 mph)	3.2 seconds
Jaguar XJ220	349 km/h	(217 mph)	3.6
Lamborghini Diablo SE30	333 km/h	(208 mph)	4.0
Ferrari F40	324 km/h	(201 mph)	4.1
Ferrari 550 Maranello	320 km/h	(199 mph)	4.3
Porsche 959	315 km/h	(198 mph)	3.6
Porsche 911 GT2	315 km/h	(198 mph)	4.1
Ferrari 456M	299 km/h	(186 mph)	5.1
Lamborghini Countach QV5000s	293 km/h	(183 mph)	4.6
Aston Martin DB7 Vantage	290 km/h	(180 mph)	5.0

MCLAREN F1

The F1 was developed by McLaren Cars Ltd, and is one of the world's fastest, most expensive road cars. And if you find a spare £600,000 at the bottom of your moneybox, there's no reason why you can't buy one! With its 6-speed manual gear transmission, the F1 has a powerful V12 BMW engine that can reach 97 km/h in 3.2 seconds! There is hardly a component in the F1 that has not been specially designed for it, mostly to save weight – the lighter the car, the faster it goes!

MEGA PEDAL
The accelerator pedal of the F1 is made up of six different titanium components alone.

FERRARI F40

Ferrari produced the F40 between 1987 and 1992, as a special supercar to celebrate the company's 40th anniversary. Early models boasted sliding windows, while the last F40s had wind-down windows and adjustable suspension. The body is made of carbon fibre so it will not rust, although it must be stored in a warm dry climate. If you look closely at the bodywork of an original F40 you should see the honeycomb weave underneath the paint. If you can't see the weave, then the car has been resprayed (some owners added an extra layer to create a perfectly smooth body).

LAMBORGHINI COUNTACH

The name Lamborghini has always been linked with quality and a tradition of excellence – no matter what the product! The original owner of the company, Ferrucio Lamborghini, started out manufacturing tractors. Today, although best known for high-performance sports cars, the bull trademark represents a massive conglomerate of businesses that produces everything from air-conditioning systems to fashion accessories and golf carts! One of the most popular sports car models, the sleek Countach QV5000S (below), became available in 1986 with a top speed of 293 km/h.

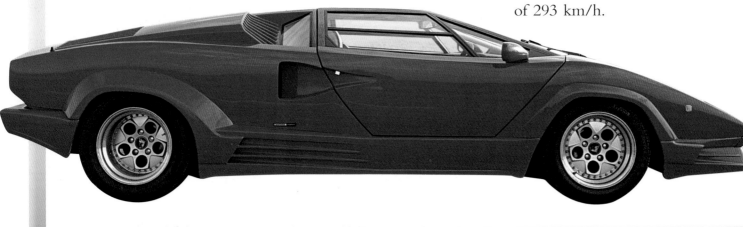

PORSCHE 911

One of the few remaining icons of the auto world, the Porsche 911 was introduced in the early 1960s, making it one of the longest-running model lines of all time. In 1999, the first all-new 911 in 30 years left the German factory. Still unmistakably a 911, the current model is longer and wider than its predecessor; however, it produces less drag and is lighter than the car it replaced. Complementing this new styling is the new engine – water cooled for the first time in 911 history.

ASTON MARTIN DB7 VANTAGE

The Aston Martin marque represents the ultimate in 'civilised' high-performance sports cars, combining traditional British styling with the latest automotive technology. From the DB2 to the racing successes of DBR1 and James Bond's DB5, these are the best-known images of Aston Martin. The latest Vantage builds on the DB7, the most successful model in the history of the British automaker. The first Aston Martin with a 12-cylinder engine, it can reach 0-97 km/h within 5 seconds; top speed is 290 km/h.

MEGA NAME
The DB of the famous Aston Martin range comes from the initials of former owner Sir David Brown, who bought the company in 1947. The most famous remains the DB5 – James Bond's car from the 1960s.

MEGA MILES
While developing the DB7 Vantage, Aston Martin made 30 prototype vehicles which covered 500,000 testing miles.

ODDBALLS

These are just a few of history's weirdest, wackiest production models, from the tiny three-wheeled bubble car to the amphicar, which can carry you over both land and water!

SINCLAIR C5

The push-button electric C5, designed by inventor Clive Sinclair, was launched in 1985. Costing £399, its body was made of the largest ever single-piece injection moulding using ICI polypropylene. But concerns regarding the C5's safety, and ridicule by the press, made the car a commercial disaster. When production ceased after just six months, only 12,000 C5s had left the factory; of these, only 10,000 were sold.

BMW ISETTA BUBBLE CAR

The bubble car arrived in the mid 1950s to take over from the motorcycle. The two main types were the Isetta and the Messerschmitt, both from Germany. These odd-looking 'bugs' could be seen everywhere, careering round corners on their three little wheels. The best news – you could drive approximately 101 km on just 4.5 litres of petrol!

MEGA SPEED
The Isetta has a top speed of 80 km/h – providing it's travelling downhill, of course!

AMPHICAR

The amphibious car or 'amphicar', as it was known, was produced by the Amphicar Corporation in Germany between 1961 and 1968. It's estimated that only some 3,700 were made, most of which were sold to the USA. Made of thick, old-fashioned steel, this 'oddball' was assembled with continuous welds and lead filling around the joins to make it completely watertight; the two doors were edged with rubber stripping. The amphicar moves in water with the use of twin nylon propellers. It can travel up to 11 km/h in water, and up to 112 km/h on land with a high-performance engine.

PEEL P50

The Peel P50 is probably the smallest motor car ever manufactured to carry an adult passenger. Constructed by the Peel Engineering Company on the Isle of Man, England, in 1962, it measures an amazing 1.34 metres in length, 99 cm in width – and just 1.34 metres in height! And with a weight of only 59 kg, you could always put it on the back of a truck and pull your Peel home if it broke down!

MEGA LIMO
One of the most outrageous cars ever is an American limousine. With 26 wheels, it's over 30 metres long. It has a swimming pool and a helicopter landing pad. When turning, it simply bends in the middle!

FUTURE FEATURES

Cars are changing, and for many reasons. Fuel shortages, dirty air, global warming – all of these factors have brought tougher government controls to the car industry. But manufacturers are already making amazing progress. Today's advances will result in cars that give fewer emissions, go farther on less fuel – and run as quiet as a mouse!

MEGA ELECTRIC

The NECAR 4 (New Electric Car, below) is powered by liquid hydrogen and has three times the range of a battery-powered vehicle. It can travel nearly 450 km before refuelling is necessary.

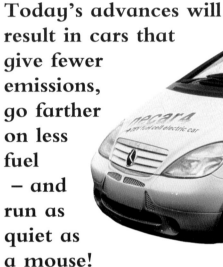

DAIMLER-BENZ F300 LIFE-JET

The amazing F300 has three wheels, two seats, a five-speed manual transmission, and a very futuristic-style body. Plus, the passenger sits behind the driver, just like on a motorcycle. Once inside the F300, with its jet-style steering wheel, instruments and gear stick, you'll think you're in an aircraft cockpit! Sensors supply data about the speed of the vehicle, its acceleration, steering wheel angle and other important information.

MEGA FAST

With a 1.6 litre petrol engine the F300 can reach a top speed of 211 km/h!

Nutty way to fuel your car!

Fuel cell-driven cars of the future could be powered by hazelnuts! Sounds nutty? Well... it's thought that hazelnuts could produce the hydrogen needed to generate an electric current for electric and hybrid cars. This is great news for Turkey, the world's largest producer of hazelnuts. The annual hazelnut harvest from this country alone could produce enough hydrogen for 2,000 cars to each travel up to 76,000 km!

MOLLER M400 SKYCAR

The M400 Skycar, built by Moller International, is capable of vertical take-off and landing, like a helicopter, and flies in a similar way to an aeroplane thanks to the aid of a special computer. And that's not all. Amazingly, the M400 can also travel short distances on the ground, like a car!

CHRYSLER CCV

Cars that are fully recyclable, with body panels made entirely from plastic mouldings, are likely to be seen in the not too distant future. In 1999 Chrysler unveiled the CCV (Composite Compact vehicle) ESX2, which is one of the most recyclable cars in the world, and can be built in just six and a half hours! Then, at the end of its life, it can be melted down and used all over again – perhaps this time becoming fizzy drinks bottles, which are made of similar plastic.

PERFECT PLASTIC!
Creation of the CCV was possible thanks to the development of new technologies that allow large panels, such as car body panels, to be formed without bending or warping.

TRUCKS

After motor cars, it was only a matter of time before trucks appeared on the scene. These vehicles soon replaced the horse-drawn cart to transport goods. Trucks are also able to travel across rough terrain that cars can not reach.

THE TRUCK CLOSE-UP

The fuel-driven truck is a wonder of modern motoring. We rely on trucks to do many different tasks. They remove our waste, deliver food to supermarkets, transport goods to countries all over the world and play a vital role in our emergency services. Let's take a closer look at the history of these transport machines and the role they play in today's world.

MEGA FACT

A truck, also called a lorry, is a motor vehicle that carries freight (goods or load). Because of their flexibility and speed, trucks now carry a quarter of all internal freight in the USA.

Trucks are classified as either straight or articulated. On a 'straight truck', axles are attached to a single frame. An articulated vehicle has two or more separate frames.

RISE OF THE LONG-HAUL TRUCK

As demand for bigger, more powerful engines grew, manufacturers like Mercedes-Benz, Cummins and Scania, turned to V8 engines. These have the advantage of more compact dimensions than in-line units. In 2000, Scania launched its R164 long haulage truck with the latest, powerful, 16-litre V8 engine.

Power is transmitted through a clutch, gearbox and differential drive. Most gearboxes have a mainshaft and twin countershafts. Many modern trucks are now automatic.

Modern trucks have electronically controlled front and rear disc brakes. Brakes are usually operated by compressed air through a system of valves. By law, all trucks must have an independent secondary system of brakes.

Some axles have the secondary reduction gearing in the wheel hubs, reducing drive-shaft stress and allowing a smaller differential housing which gives improved ground clearance. The drive from the gearbox to the rear axle is transmitted by a propeller shaft with universal joints.

PETROL VERSUS DIESEL

Until the 1930s, the petrol engine was widely used for trucks, especially in the USA. Since World War II, diesel-powered engines have become more popular for trucks used on heavy, long-distance hauls. Diesel trucks are often more costly than similar models using petrol-burning engines, but they are more efficient burners of fuel.

TRUCKS TAKE TO THE ROAD

Early road transport depended on the horse-drawn cart. The first steam-powered vehicle was built in 1769 by French military engineer, Nicholas Joseph Cugnot. His three-wheeled steam machine ran for fifteen minutes at about 10 km/h. The vehicle was driven through the front wheel and the weight of the mechanisms made it difficult to steer. In 1803, in England, Richard Trevithick produced a steam carriage to transport passengers from central to west London.

THORNYCROFT

Designed in 1864, the Thornycroft steam-powered van wasn't built until 1896. With a one-tonne payload the van was displayed at the 1898 Crystal Palace Show in London, England. Thornycroft's steam-powered traction engines had also been used to pull loads and to drive machinery. As one of the world's first load-bearing, commercial vehicles, it is closest form of transport to the modern truck.

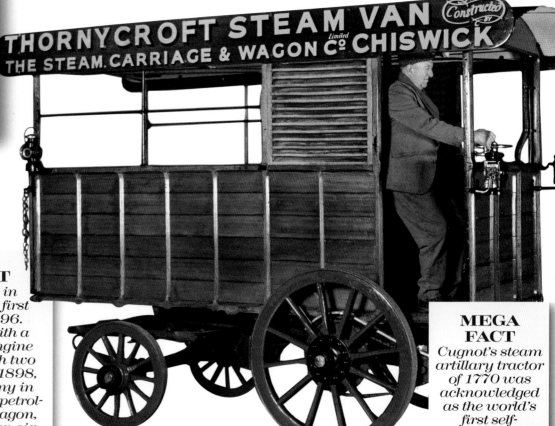

MEGA FACT
Gottlieb Daimler in Germany built the first motor truck in 1896. It was equipped with a four-horsepower engine and a belt drive with two speeds forward. In 1898, the Winton Company in the USA produced a petrol-powered delivery wagon, with a single-cylinder, six-horsepower engine.

MEGA FACT
Cugnot's steam artillary tractor of 1770 was acknowledged as the world's first self-propelled road vehicle.

LACRE MOTOR CAR

The Lacre Motor Car Company began producing cars and light vans in 1902. From 1909, Lacre, which derived its name from an abbreviation of Long Acre in London, where it was based, began producing

trucks up to 9 tonnes payload capacity. During World War I, Lacre focused on building military vehicles. After the war, the company switched to manufacturing road sweepers. Load-carrying trucks continued to be produced until the company wound up in 1928.

MEGA WEIRD
Under the Locomotives on Highways Act of 1861, all mechanical vehicles in Britain needed an attendant to walk 55 metres in front carrying a red flag! The speed limit was 3 km/h in towns, while 6.5 km/h was allowed on rural highways.

In 1907, the upmarket Harrods store in Brompton Road, London, used this early Lacre van to deliver goods to their wealthy customers. Trucks now had air suspension and electric lighting instead of paraffin and acetylene. Bigger, heavier trucks also had pneumatic tyres, which made for a more comfortable ride.

THE FIRST LEYLAND VAN

Leyland began in 1896 when James Sumner and the Spurrier family founded the Lancashire Steam Motor Company in the town of Leyland, in north-west England. In the same year, with the help of 20 employees, Sumner completed his first vehicle – a 1.5-tonne-capacity steam wagon, with oil-fired boiler, cart wheels and tiller steering. It was the start of what was to become an unbeaten heritage of engineering and outstanding production performance that has made today's Leyland trucks popular.

MEGA FACT
Although pneumatic tyres appeared on vehicles as early as 1904, large trucks still used hard rubber tyres until World War I. Cotton was replaced by synthetics in the carcass of truck tyres in the 1930s, with steel wire and fibreglass plies appearing later.

'Pig' was the name given to Leyland's first petrol-engined truck. An improved model appeared in 1905, with production reaching 16 chassis.

MEGA FACT
In 1897, German engineer Rudolph Diesel demonstrated the first diesel engine.

ALBION

Founded in 1899, the Albion Motor Car Company produced its first commercial vehicle, a half-tonne van, in 1902. In 1910, Albion produced their A10 truck for three to four-tonne payloads. This had a four-cylinder petrol engine and chain drive. Albion built six thousand of these trucks for service in World War 1. The company also supplied military trucks during World War II, producing three-tonne 4x4s, 10-tonne 6x4s and heavy-duty tank transporters. In 1951, Albion was taken over by Leyland Motors, and most of Albion's heavy trucks were phased out.

Foden

Foden Limited started life when Hancock and Foden began building agricultural machinery and steam engines in 1856. In 1887, Edwin Foden demonstrated a prototype (first model) steam

traction engine. By 1901, Foden's steam truck was cruising at 10 km/h. The company reluctantly stopped producing steam trucks in 1934 due to the popularity of internal-combustion-engined trucks.

Big rigs, such as Freightliners, are among the most powerful trucks. Trains for these trucks can weigh between 500 to 1000 tonnes, and up to four tractors can be coupled together to provide the tractive effort. Tractors are powered by turbo-charged and after-cooled diesel engines and can weigh up to 40 tonnes each.

BIG RIGS

The lack of roads and waterways encouraged the Australians to create the monster-long 'road train'. This solved the problem of transporting supplies across the country.

SCANIA HEAVY ARCTIC

With its new cab design and low-emission diesel powers, this R144 articulated truck from Scania's model 4 series has a 14-litre engine capacity. The prefix 'R' indicates a full-height cab (as this picture shows), 'P' indicates a low-profile cab and 'T' a bonneted cab. Celebrating its centenary in 1991, it took Scania 75 years to build its first 1,000,000 vehicles. Vehicle number 500,000 was made in 1987 – 96 years after the company was founded. But it took just 13 years to build the next half million – by the year 2000!

> **MEGA FACT**
> A driver's working day is well documented with modern technology. A tachograph reveals the number of hours driven, and at what speed. A GPS satellite monitoring system lets traffic dispatchers know exactly where each truck is located.

AUSSIE ROAD TRAIN

These trucks are only found in Australia and were originally produced to service far-flung communities. Around five per cent of the total transportation in Australia takes place via road trains. Rigs have huge trailer combinations measuring up to 53 metres in length. Rigs carry around 140 tonnes each – equivalent to 400 head of cattle or 125,000 litres of aviation fuel. Scania's 480 and 580 hp 16-litre V8 engines are capable of high average speeds at modest fuel consumption. The Scania 470 hp 12-litre turbo-compound engine is another truck often used for road-train deliveries in the outback.

MONSTER TRUCKS

The Monster truck was born when a few enthusiasts in the 1970s began making their pickups bigger and better by adding huge tyres and faster engines. The first Monster truck was Bigfoot, built from a Ford F250 pick-up truck. In the early 1980s, chrome-crunching monsters appeared at motor sports events and fairs, where they were rolled over cars with the sole intention of flattening them. By the mid-1980s, car crushing gave way to racing.

BIGGER AND BETTER

Huge 170-cm tall tyres and alcohol-injected engines generate over 1,500hp, making today's monster trucks bigger, tougher and meaner than ever.

MEGA FACT
Most Monster trucks are magnificent beasts, weighing a minimum of 4,500 kg. A monster truck is around 3 metres tall and 3.5 metres wide.

MEGA WEIRD
Monster trucks are built for short, high-powered bursts of speed. They generate an average of 1,500 to 2,000 hp and are capable of up to 160 km/h. These huge trucks can jump 35-38 metres (more than 14 cars side by side) and up to eight metres in the air.

Monster Rollover

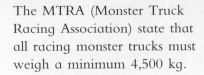

Overkill, from Fort Wayne, Indiana, USA, is one of the lightest trucks on the American circuits.

The MTRA (Monster Truck Racing Association) state that all racing monster trucks must weigh a minimum 4,500 kg.

Overkill, which weighs 90 kg under the limit, must have weights added to it in order to keep its tyres on the ground.

MEGA FACT

Built in 1991, Snake Bite competed in the USA on the PENDA points series until 1994. The latest model, a 1997 Ford, has a 572ci Ford Hemi engine, a GTS fibreglass body and a custom nose. Its flashing eyes and snake fangs are highlighted by a custom 'scaled' paint scheme. Snake Bite was the first Monster Truck to be retro-fitted with a fibreglass body .

MONSTER TRUCKS

CAROLINA CRUSHER

The first Carolina Crusher was built in North Carolina, USA, in 1985. Since then, these 'monsters' have been improved with each successive model. Some of the older Carolina Crusher's were sold to English promoters, and now have new names. One is called the Bandit, and tours across the UK.

MEGA MILITARY
The first side-by-side monster truck race took place in 1992. Instead of racing against the clock, these huge beasts raced head to head!

PURE ADRENALIN

The chassis on this 2000 Ford Super Duty truck was especially built to accommodate the John Hutcherson Custom Turbo 400 Transmission and 557 cubic inch Fontana Hemi engine. Weighing 4,672 kg, this up-to-the-minute monster made its debut in April 2000, entering the first pro MT (professional MonsterTruck) race in South Carolina, USA. In 2001, Pure Adrenalin went on to take third place in the pro MT race series, competing against such fearsome foes as Bigfoot.

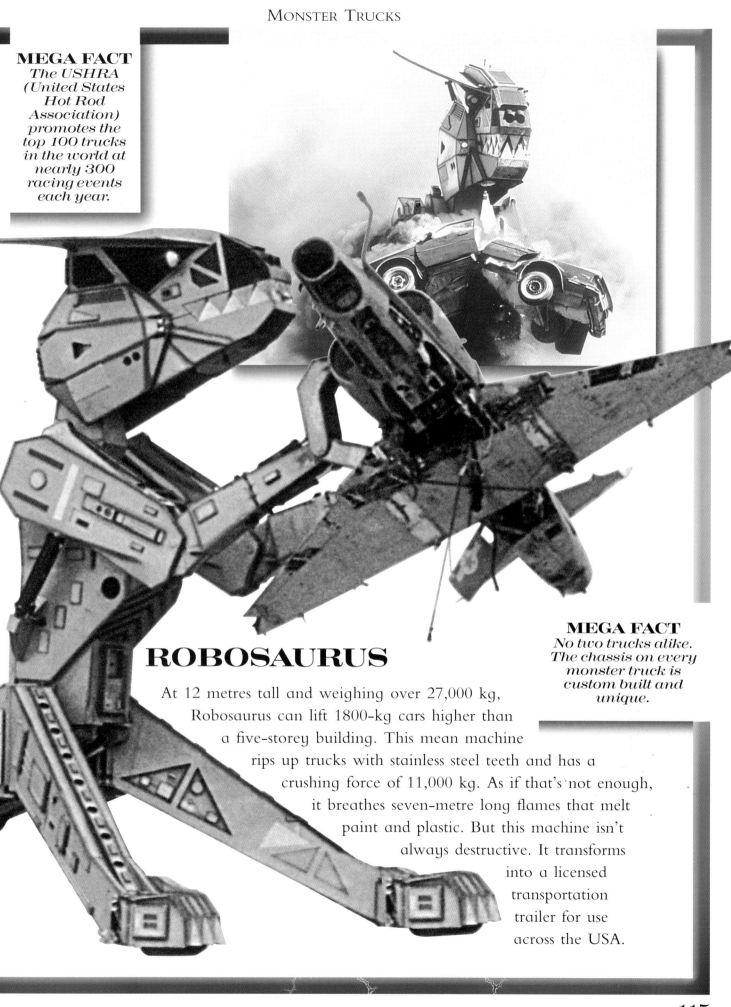

ROBOSAURUS

At 12 metres tall and weighing over 27,000 kg,
Robosaurus can lift 1800-kg cars higher than
a five-storey building. This mean machine
rips up trucks with stainless steel teeth and has a
crushing force of 11,000 kg. As if that's not enough,
it breathes seven-metre long flames that melt
paint and plastic. But this machine isn't
always destructive. It transforms
into a licensed
transportation
trailer for use
across the USA.

SPECIALISED TRUCKS

Basic truck bodies can only be adapted up to a limit. This is why purpose-built models are needed for many tasks for which trucks are used today. These jobs include transporting loads, such as timber logs and hazardous chemicals, putting out fires and lifting heavy objects. Specialised trucks are designed to cope with almost every kind of hauling job.

TWO FOR ONE

Caterpillar grew from the 1925 merger of two American agricultural equipment manufactures, Holt Manufacturing Company and the C L Best Gas Traction Company.

GOOD SOLUTION

Benjamin Holt produced agricultural equipment, such as combine harvesters that used steam-traction engines to pull them through the fields. These heavy engines often sank into the ground. In 1904, Holt tested the first practical crawler tractor. He removed the rear drive wheels from a Holt Junior Road Engine and replaced them with a pair of tracks, three metres long and 60 cm wide.

Truck Fest

Truck Fest is Europe's biggest truck show, an annual meeting event for the Road Haulage Industry, as well as buyers and enthusiasts. Highlights include stunt action from the best Monster Trucks, and competitions to find the best new truck, the best working truck, the best vintage truck and even best paintwork.

SPECIALISED TRUCKS

ARMOURED

Trucks play a major part in military operations all over the world and have been used by the armed forces since World War I. Oshkosh Truck Corporation is one of the leading manufacturers of specialised military trucks. Protected from gunfire and even landmines, armoured trucks are now able to go into more dangerous areas that were often avoided.

MEGA WEIRD
Armies carry equipment in amphibious trucks that are able to drive on land and float on water. To stop water flooding the engine, these trucks have a waterproof underside.

CONCRETE MIXER

Many of today's concrete mixers are 6x4s with drum capacities of six to seven cubic metres. Some larger multi-axle mixers have drum capacities of between 12 and 15 cubic metres. Modern concrete mixers, often called 'readymix' trucks, have a separate engine to turn the drum at different speeds. Some have a P T O (power take-off) which allows auxiliary equipment to be driven off the vehicle's gearbox or engine.

MEGA FACT
To learn to drive large goods vehicles you must be at least 21 years old and hold a full standard driving licence.

TANKER

There are two basic types of tanker – those that carry bulk liquids and those for bulk powders. Bulk liquid tankers have been built since the early 1920s. The early vehicles had rectangular bodies. Cylindrical and elliptical barrels followed later, with better manufacturing techniques. Bulk powder tankers have only been made since the 1950s. Some tanks consist of one compartment, while others can have five or more separate compartments for different products. When carrying dangerous chemicals, strict safety codes are applied and drivers must have special training.

FIRE TRUCK

Fire trucks have advanced dramatically since open appliances with warning bells roared through our streets, with the crew clinging onto their sides. Long after most trucks began using diesel engines, fire trucks continued to use petrol, which gave faster acceleration. Scania export their fire trucks to countries all over the world. One of the reasons for Scania's success is their specially designed CrewCab for advanced emergency-rescue applications.

SPECIALISED TRUCKS

RECOVERY TRUCK

Modern recovery trucks are capable of removing a vehicle weighing up to 50 tonnes. In the past, most recovery trucks used a crane jib to lift a vehicle. With engine sizes reaching 500bhp, tow trucks today are likely to come fitted with an innovative 12-tonne underlift capability. This is a powerful hydraulic boom that can be extended under the truck to support the front axle. Self-loading, lightweight trucks are still used by small garages and private users.

LOGGING TRUCK

There are two classes of logging truck – those that operate on public roads and those restricted to private forestry areas. Only those trucks travelling on public roads have to conform to length and weight limits. Companies including Kenworth, Mack, Scania and Volvo produce huge, high-powered tractors designed specifically for the logging industry. Special trailers with bolsters are used to carry logs. Larger trucks can haul three or more trailers, each carrying around 50 tonnes.

GARBAGE TRUCK

Gone are the days of the covered dump truck, built with just a standard chassis and a hatch through which refuse could be emptied. With the huge increase in household refuse (waste) in the last 30 to 40 years, massive three and four-axled trucks at up to 32 tonnes gvw (gross vehicle weight) are now used. These trucks have automatic transmission and the latest hydraulic compression equipment.

MOBILE CRANE

Today, most cranes are purpose-built and highly specialised, but early mobile cranes were mounted on truck chassis. Cranes with lifting capacities from 10 to 100 tonnes are often adequate, although there are companies, such as Krupp, that produce a crane with a lifting capacity for 1000 tonnes!

4x4 – OFF ROAD

At one time, the only trucks to have four-wheel drive, also known as 4WD or 4x4, were 'off-road' vehicles such as Jeeps and military vehicles. These machines were designed to travel over rough, muddy terrain (land), which would be impossible for two-wheel drive vehicles. Modern 4x4 trucks are becoming popular because of their efficiency, stability on cornering and easy maneuverability. Four-wheel drive SUTs (Sports Utility Trucks), which are often seen on city roads, combine the latest technology and high-performance with stylish good looks.

MEGA INFO
Understanding what veteran SUV enthusiasts are talking about can sometimes be confusing! Here are a few terms to help you keep up with the jargon!

2WD = Two-Wheel Drive
4WD = Four-Wheel Drive
AWD = All-Wheel Drive
GVWR = Gross Vehicle Weight Rating
GAWR = Gross Axle Weight Rating
GCWR = Gross Combined Weight Rating

FOUR-WHEEL

On four-wheel drive trucks, such as the Hummer, the engine makes all the wheels turn. This gives more stability when travelling at speed, especially in poor conditions, such as snow and rain.

TWO-WHEEL DRIVE

Two-wheel drive vehicles are either 'front' wheel drive or 'rear' wheel drive. This means that only the two front wheels or back wheels move the vehicle along. If too much power is applied to these driving wheels or the road surface is slippery, then the tyres can easily lose their grip.

Hummer on Ice

The typical 4WD system comprises of a gearbox, a transfer box that selects the power to either two- or four-wheel drives, and two sets of driving axles or drive shafts. On 4WDs, all four wheels can be driven all of the time, or just some of the time. There are normally two positions for 4WD: 'High 4' is used for dusty, dirt or wet roads, and 'Low 4' is used on snow, sand or mud surfaces at much slower speeds.

MULTIPLE HUMMERS

The Hummer was originally designed as an all-purpose vehicle for the American Armed Forces, where it is known as the Humvee. The Hummer went on sale to the public in October 1992. Available in two-door Hard Top, four-door Hard Top, Open Top and Wagon, the Hummer goes from 0-95 km/h in just 16 seconds, with a top speed of around 135 km/h. A Central Tyre Inflation System now allows the driver to inflate or deflate the tyres from inside the vehicle.

MEGA FACT

Since 1999, the Hummer's standard traction-control system means that running soft tyres may be in the past. TorqTrac4 uses sensors on all wheels to monitor wheel slip. If wheel speed exceeds vehicle speed, the system applies braking to the spinning wheel and transfers torque to the wheels that still have some grip.

4x4 – OFF ROAD

CHRYSLER JEEP CHEROKEE

The Cherokee was introduced to British buyers in the early 1990s, when there was an increase in demand for 4x4 transport.

The Grand Cherokee 4.0 Limited was launched in 1996. With full time 4WD, cruise control, central locking, air conditioning, electric windows and mirrors, heated electric front seats, twin airbags, alarm and immobiliser, this truck has practically every modern convenience you can think of.

LAND ROVER DISCOVERY

In 1948, the first prototype Land-Rovers were built on Jeep chassis. As steel was scarce after World War II, the body was made of an aluminium alloy. Land Rover Discovery I was released in the UK in 1989 to fill the gap between the Range Rover and Land Rover Defender. It had permanent 4WD, four doors and the option of a diesel engine.

4X4 PICK-UP

In 1948, Ford introduced what has become one of their best-selling trucks – the Ford F150 Regular Cab Pick-Up. This sturdy, reliable vehicle was intended to meet all the demands of the work-truck user, while comfortably seating three people. The F150 SuperCab, launched in 1974, provided a larger cab with a small rear-seat area for luggage or occasional six-passenger transportation. The Ford F-Series has been the best-selling truck in the USA for more than twenty years.

FORD EXPLORER

The Ford Explorer 4.0, a good seller in the USA, was launched in the UK in 1997. With a petrol-guzzling 4008cc engine, this 4x4 will do around 20-25mpg. The truck comes with a five-speed automatic transmission, full-time 4WD and self-levelling rear suspension.

AIRCRAFT

It is difficult to imagine travelling abroad without going on an aeroplane. Aircraft have made our world a much smaller place. Countries that once took days, months, even years to reach are now accessible within a matter of hours!

THE PLANE CLOSE-UP

Many different planes have been designed and built since the first powered aircraft took off a hundred years ago. On the following pages you'll find classic designs, mega powerful jets and discover how the story of aviation developed.

THE COMPONENTS

A small propeller-driven aeroplane may look very different from a powerful modern jetliner but all planes are the same in some ways and are made of similar components. These components – including the engine, wings and control surfaces – are there to help make a plane fly.

This big aeroplane is a passenger airliner. It is powered by four jet engines. Two engines are attached to each wing.

MEGA UPLIFTING
Sir George Cayley (1773-1857) was the first to show how wings with a curved top edge work better. He showed that faster air flowing over the top of a wing has less pressure. This means that slower air beneath the wings has greater pressure and so pushes the plane up into the air.

Nose wheels, part of the undercarriage.

The flight deck, where the captain and first officer sit. A flight engineer sits behind them.

The fuselage, or main body, of a small aircraft is usually a single shell. Larger airliners, like this commercial jet, need braces to add extra strength to the body.

The Flight Deck

The first planes had a few simple instruments to help the pilot fly. Today, the cockpit is full of dials and screens called CRTs (or cathode ray tubes, like TV monitors). These give pilots all the information they need, including speed, altitude and direction. There are also radar screens and map displays, and lamps light up to warn the pilot of any problems.

The tailplane keeps the aircraft stable in flight. Elevators on the tail fin are raised to make the plane climb. The rudder on the tail fin moves to steer the plane to the left or right.

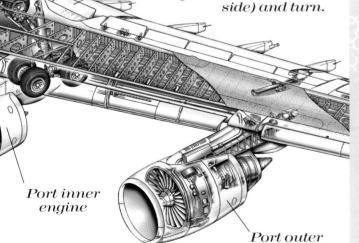

Ailerons on the wings are raised and lowered to make the plane roll (lean to the side) and turn.

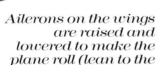

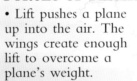

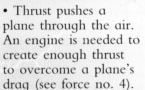

Port inner engine

Port outer engine

FORCES OF FLIGHT

- Lift pushes a plane up into the air. The wings create enough lift to overcome a plane's weight.

1

- Thrust pushes a plane through the air. An engine is needed to create enough thrust to overcome a plane's drag (see force no. 4).

2

- The plane's weight is a negative force, pulling it down to earth.

3

- The negative force of drag is caused by air resistance. It tries to slow a plane down.

4

FIRST FLIGHTS

At the very beginning of the 20th century, two American bicycle-makers built their own full-size gliders, as well as a specially designed petrol engine. Then they put all their expertise together to build the world's first successful powered aeroplane, which they called *Flyer*. The two men were brothers – Wilbur and Orville Wright – the pioneers of aviation.

The picture below shows a fine replica of the Wrights' Flyer.

Wright Brothers' Flyer

MEGA WOODEN

Flyer's airframe was made of ash and spruce wood. The wooden wings were covered with linen and stiffened with bracing wires.

This famous photo shows the moment when Flyer first took off from its guide rail, with Orville Wright as pilot while Wilbur looks on.

Leonardo Da Vinci

Four hundred years before the Wright brothers' success, a great Italian painter, sculptor and scientist designed several flying machines. Leonardo da Vinci (1452-1519) bought caged birds in the market and then set them free. He studied the way they flew and drew up his own ideas for human flight. The pilot was supposed to lie down in this machine, called an ornithopter. Leonardo's ideas were brilliant for the time, but his flying machines never flew.

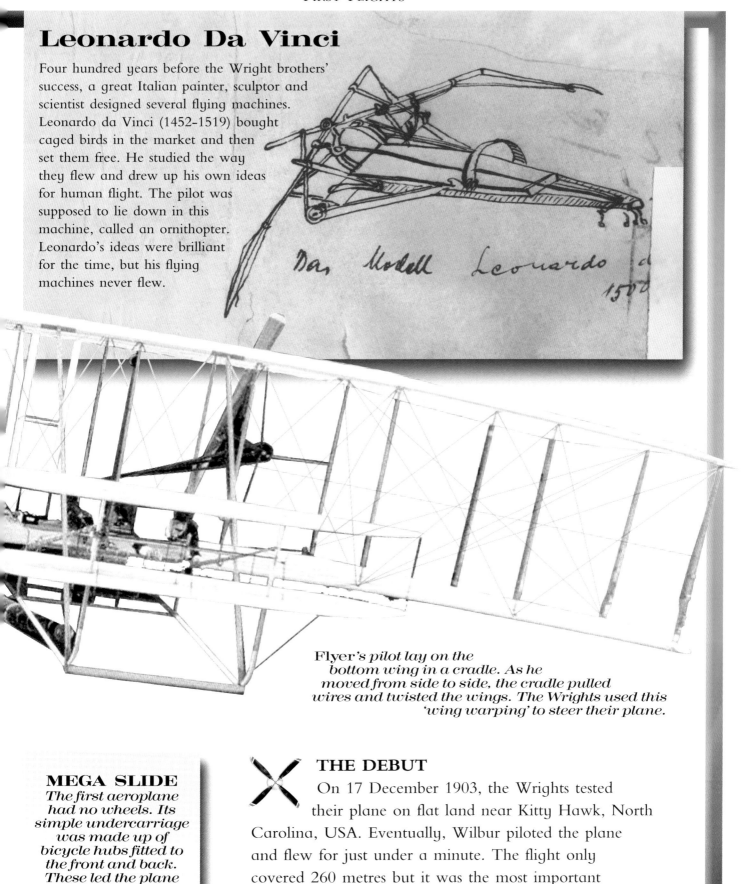

Flyer's pilot lay on the bottom wing in a cradle. As he moved from side to side, the cradle pulled wires and twisted the wings. The Wrights used this 'wing warping' to steer their plane.

MEGA SLIDE
The first aeroplane had no wheels. Its simple undercarriage was made up of bicycle hubs fitted to the front and back. These led the plane along an 18-metre wooden launching rail until it gained enough speed and lift to take off.

THE DEBUT

On 17 December 1903, the Wrights tested their plane on flat land near Kitty Hawk, North Carolina, USA. Eventually, Wilbur piloted the plane and flew for just under a minute. The flight only covered 260 metres but it was the most important event in aviation history.

131

FIRST FLIGHTS

BLÉRIOT TYPE XI

On 25 July 1909 French aviator Louis Blériot (1872-1936) made the world's first international flight. He took up a newspaper challenge to fly over the English Channel from France to England, and won £1000 (then a great deal of money!) when he made it in his Type XI monoplane. He landed near Dover Castle 36 minutes after taking off from Les Baraques in France. This historic flight made Blériot an overnight celebrity, and more than a hundred of his Type XIs were ordered and built.

MEGA HORSEPOWER
The Type XI's wooden propeller was driven by a motorcycle engine. This produced 25hp — twice as much as the Wrights' Flyer — but it was still only just enough power to get across the Channel.

LILIENTHAL GLIDER

German engineer Otto Lilienthal (1848-96) was another of the great pioneers of aviation. He made more than 2,000 flights with his own gliders, which were rather like modern hang-gliders. He steered by shifting his weight forwards and backwards, and from side to side. Newspapers called him the 'flying man', but he had to be a tough man too, because he crashed many times. He was eventually killed when his glider crashed on a hillside near Berlin.

MEGA GLIDE
Otto Lilienthal ran along and took off from hilltops. His record glide carried him along for 350 metres.

MEGA LAUNCH
Otto Lilienthal performed most of his gliding from a man-made hill he constructed near his home in Germany.

VICKERS VIMY

The sturdy Vickers Vimy broke all kinds of records, including first across the Atlantic, first from Europe to Australia and first from Britain to South Africa. The journey from England to Australia took 29 days, with many stopovers on the way. This bi-plane was designed during World War I as a bomber. As soon as the war was over, many were converted to civilian use because they were so strong and reliable. The Vimy was just over 13 metres long with a wingspan of nearly 21 metres. Like all early planes, it had an open cockpit for the two-man crew.

First Across the Atlantic

In 1918 an English newspaper offered a prize of £10,000 to the first person to fly non-stop across the Atlantic Ocean. On 14 June 1919 two English airmen, Captain John Alcock (1892-1919) and Lieutenant Arthur Whitten Brown (1886-1948), shown right, took off in their Vickers Vimy bi-plane from the North American coast. Sixteen and a half hours later, pilot Alcock and navigator Brown landed in Ireland, freezing cold and nose-down in a peat bog! Both men were knighted, but tragically Sir John Alcock was killed just six months after his transatlantic flight in a flying accident in France. It was not until 1927 that a solo transatlantic flight was achieved when Charles Lindbergh (1902-74) flew from New York to Paris. His small Ryan monoplane, *Spirit of St. Louis*, achieved an average speed of 173 km/h.

PROP CLASSICS

In the 1930s aircraft manufacturers started designing planes specially for carrying passengers. The new airlines wanted to attract customers by offering a service that was better than long-distance trains over land or ships across the sea. So they had to make their planes bigger, faster and more comfortable than they were before.

THE DOUGLAS DC-3

The Douglas DC-3 (below) was an early airliner, and it went on to become one of the most successful planes ever built. It first went into service in 1936, and of the 11,000 DC-3s that were made, some are still flying today. The controls on the DC-3 included an automatic pilot and two sets of instruments.

MEGA MILITARY
By 1939, 90 per cent of the USA's air passengers were flying on DC-2s and DC-3s. Their versatility also led to the use of DC-3s in World War II. Known as Skytrains or Skytroopers, they were mass-produced for the military and were used as freight and personnel carriers, ambulances and even glider tugs.

The three-bladed propellers were driven by 1100hp Wright Cyclone engines. Compare that with Blériot's 25hp!

MERCER

MEGA SNOOZE
The first version of the DC-3 took off as a DST, or Douglas Sleeper Transport. There were 14 sleeping bunks for passengers on overnight flights. Later versions of the plane were called Douglas Dakotas.

The two main undercarriage legs and wheels were raised up into the engine houses after take-off. This helped streamlining and was a new feature in the 1930s.

Flying in the 1930s

This Flying Banana airliner waits for its passengers (38 at most!) at Croydon Airport, south of London. Imperial Airways, which was the first British national airline, was founded in 1924. Croydon was a very advanced airport for its time. In the 1930s many others were still made up of huts and tents. At all airports, passengers had to walk to their plane – there were no jetways or shuttle buses.

DC-3s had a cruise speed of 274 km/h.

The DC-3 was almost 20 metres long and had a wingspan of 29 metres. It was made from an alloy skin over an alloy frame, joined together by metal rivets.

HOME COMFORTS

In the DC-3, for the first time, up to 28 passengers enjoyed comfortable seats, ventilation and heating. There was a galley for preparing drinks and food, and a toilet. Air travel was certainly improving, and there was even the added service of a stewardess.

PROP CLASSICS

BOEING 247

Boeing was one of the first great aircraft companies. Its founder, William Boeing, learned to fly in 1915 and then started an airmail service between the USA and Canada. In 1933 Boeing introduced his own new aircraft, the 247. This was the world's first streamlined metal airliner, carrying ten passengers and 180 kilograms of mail. It took the 247 20 hours to fly between New York and Los Angeles – 7.5 hours faster than any previous airliners! The 247's two Wasp engines drove adjustable propellers. These allowed the pilot to set the blades at the best angle for a particular speed.

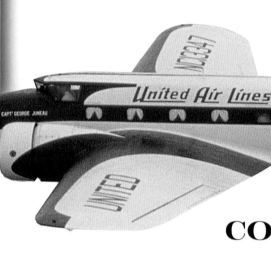

LOCKHEED CONSTELLATION

The Constellation first took to the air in 1938, but it really developed as a commercial airliner after 1945. It had four propeller engines and was one of the first airliners to have a nosewheel instead of a tailwheel, so that the passenger cabin was level with the ground. Lockheed developed more and more different versions of the Constellation, concentrating on comfort. Some had reclining sleeper seats, while others had a luxurious cocktail lounge on board.

MEGA DISTANCE
Lockheed Constellations were used on long-distance routes. In 1946 they were the first planes to fly across the Atlantic from the USA to London's new Heathrow airport.

Amelia Earhart

In 1932, the American aviator Amelia Earhart became the first woman to fly solo across the Atlantic, in a Lockheed Vega. By then she had already helped found an international group of women pilots called the 'Ninety-Nines'. Three years later, she was the first woman to fly solo across the Pacific, from Hawaii to California. Then, in 1937, Earhart tried to fly around the world in a twin-engined Lockheed Electra, with the help of a navigator, Fred Noonan. The plane vanished over the Pacific, but no wreckage has ever been found. The mystery of Amelia Earhart's disappearance has yet to be solved.

HANDLEY PAGE HP42

Do you think the fuselage of the HP42 looks a bit like a banana? Well, that was the nickname of this famous airliner – the Flying Banana. The first Banana (registration code G-AAGX, as shown here) took off in 1940. But although they were very popular with passengers, only eight of these bi-planes were ever built. The strange layout of the engines, with two on the upper and two on the lower wing, was supposed to cut down noise inside the passenger cabin. Each upholstered seat had its own heating and ventilation controls – the height of luxury.

MEGA SLOW
The HP42 was designed for comfort, not speed. Flights from England to India took six days, and those to South Africa eight and a half days!

137

MILITARY MACHINES

Propeller-driven planes played an important part in World War I (1914-18), and aircraft engineers learned a lot about what planes could do. By World War II (1939-45), the invention of the jet engine had changed things dramatically. Jet fighters were much faster, but they were not used in great numbers and so did not have a great effect on the war itself. Nevertheless, the age of the jet was with us.

WWI SOPWITH CAMEL

The Camel was one of the greatest fighter planes of World War I. Flying at up to 185 km/h, it was faster than most other fighters, but its powerful 150hp engine made it difficult to fly. The pilot sat in a wicker seat and had to turn the plane to face its target before firing his machine-guns. Like most aircraft of the time, the Camel was a bi-plane.

MEGA SUCCESS
The Sopwith Camel only entered World War I in 1917, but it was the most successful British fighter. A total of 5,490 Camels were built, and they claimed no fewer than 1,294 victories over German aircraft.

The Camel's wings and fuselage were made of a wooden frame covered with canvas.

Twin machine-guns on the Sopwith Camel were fired between the propeller blades. The guns fired straight ahead; they could not swivel.

Four 30-mm guns fired through slots in the nose of the Me 262.

The Messerschmitt's bubble canopy gave the single pilot good all-round vision.

The Me 262 measured 10.5 metres long and had a wingspan of 12.5 metres.

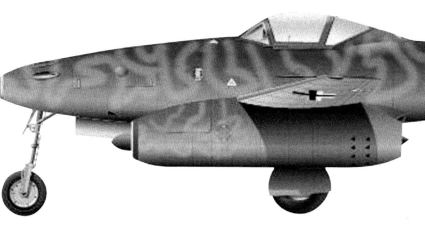

Bombs could be carried under the Messerschmitt's fuselage.

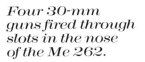 WW2 MESSERSCHMITT ME 262

This famous German fighter plane was designed by Willy Messerschmitt (1898–1978). Powered by two turbojet engines, the plane first flew in 1942. Two years later it became the first jet aircraft in the world to go into full military service. The Me 262 had a top speed of 868 km/h – that's more than four times faster than the Sopwith Camel! It proved to be rather unreliable, however, and many Me 262s crashed.

MEGA QUICK LEARNER
The Camel was designed and built by Sir Thomas Octave Murdoch Sopwith (1888-1989). In 1910 he took up flying, and on 21 November he sat in a bi-plane for the first time. By tea-time he had qualified for his Pilot's Certificate. The following month, he won a special prize for the longest distance flown in a straight line .

The Camel had a tail skid instead of a rear wheel.

FIRST JET ENGINE

English engineer Sir Frank Whittle (1907–96) began work on a jet engine in 1928, while he was a student at the Royal Air Force College in Cranwell. By 1935 he had developed a prototype, and two years later he built and ran the world's first aircraft jet engine. It was fitted to a Gloster Meteor fighter in 1941. By 1944 the RAF were flying squadrons of Meteor jets.

The Sopwith Camel was nearly 6 metres long and had a wingspan of 8.5 metres.

MILITARY MACHINES

AVRO LANCASTER

The Lancaster was a heavy British bomber used in World War II. It was a four-engined development of the earlier twin-engined Avro Manchester. A modified version of the Lancaster was used in the famous dam-busting raids on northern Germany in 1943. They dropped special bouncing bombs to hit the dams and destroy them. 'Lancs' were also used to lead large groups of bombers on big missions.

> ### MEGA MISSIONS
> *In 1943 and 1944, a Lancaster plane nicknamed 'The Mother of Them All' flew on 140 missions, more than any other bomber.*

SUPERMARINE SPITFIRE

The Spitfire is one of the best-known propeller-driven fighters of all time. It first flew in 1936 and stayed in production right through World War II. By 1945 more than 20,000 Spitfires had been built, and many took part in dogfights during the Battle of Britain. The original Spitfire had a top speed of 571 km/h, while the later Spitfire Mark XIX could fly at 718 km/h.

BAe HARRIER JUMP JET

The Harrier fighter bomber first went into service with the Royal Air Force in 1969. It is a 'jump jet' or VTOL (vertical take-off and landing) aircraft, which means it can take off straight upwards, hover and land straight down. To make this possible, the Harrier has special moveable engine nozzles. During normal flight they point backwards, but they can swivel to point downwards and make VTOL possible.

LOCKHEED F-117 NIGHTHAWK

The F-117 Nighthawk bomber is a stealth aircraft. This means that it is specially designed to be very difficult to detect with radar or sonar equipment. The Nighthawk's unusual shape, with many different flat surfaces, helps make this possible by breaking up radar waves. The Lockheed F-117 was first shown in public in 1990. Like all modern military aircraft, many of its features are kept secret. One thing we do know: the Nighthawk is sprayed with special material to absorb radar. The plane is 20 metres long, just and has a wingspan of 13 metres.

THE JETS

The first jet planes took to the skies in 1939, and a few were used as fighters during World War II. Jets could fly much faster and higher than propeller-driven planes, and during the 1950s jet airliners – or jetliners – went into service with the world's growing airlines. They made long flights quicker and more comfortable, and before long they could carry more than a hundred passengers each.

RUNWAY REQUIREMENTS

Big aircraft need big airports. As larger, heavier jetliners have been introduced, airports have had to lengthen their runways to make sure they have plenty of room for take-off and landing. A 747, for example, needs over 3 km of runway to reach its take-off speed.

Winglets curve up at the end of the wings. They help to reduce drag. The Boeing 747-400 has a wingspan of 64.4 metres.

This jumbo is powered by 4 turbofan jet engines, attached to the wings by pylons. Leading-edge flaps at the front of the wings come out during take-off and landing. These give the plane extra lift at low speeds.

MEGA JOURNEY
The 747SP long-range jumbo jet flies the world's longest non-stop route, the 12,050-km, 15-hour trip from Los Angeles to Sydney.

Inside a Jet Engine

Jet engines produce tremendous thrust. The engine sucks in air at the front, and a machine called a compressor raises the air's pressure. This compressed air is then sprayed with aircraft fuel, and the mixture is lit by an electric spark. The burning gases quickly expand and blast out through the back of the engine. As the jets of gas shoot backwards, the aircraft is thrust forwards.

There are different kinds of jet engine. Most of today's airliners are powered by turbofans, like the one shown below. This has a large fan at the front, which helps to suck in air. Turbofans are quieter than other jet engines, burning fuel more efficiently and giving more thrust at low speeds.

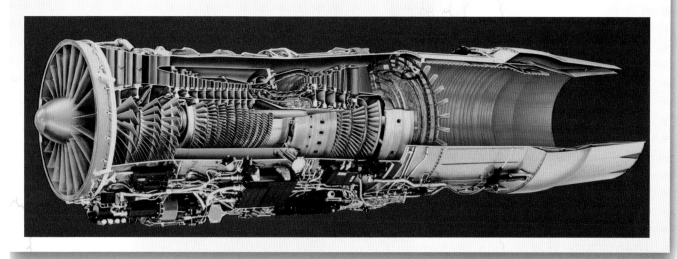

The passengers at the front of the plane are sitting beneath the flight deck, which is on the upper floor.

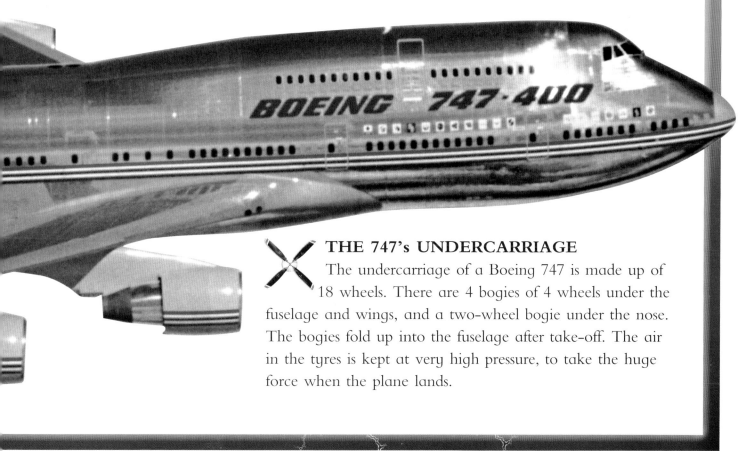

THE 747's UNDERCARRIAGE

The undercarriage of a Boeing 747 is made up of 18 wheels. There are 4 bogies of 4 wheels under the fuselage and wings, and a two-wheel bogie under the nose. The bogies fold up into the fuselage after take-off. The air in the tyres is kept at very high pressure, to take the huge force when the plane lands.

143

THE JETS

CONCORDE

Concorde was the world's only supersonic passenger aircraft. It was developed by British and French engineers and went into service with British Airways and Air France in 1976. Travelling faster than the speed of sound meant that Concorde could fly from New York to London in less than three hours. Only 16 Concordes were ever built. After a crash in 2000 they were grounded while safety tests were carried out, but took to the skies once again in November 2001. However, Concorde flew its last commercial passenger flight in October 2003.

MEGA NOSY
In supersonic flight, Concorde's nose points straight ahead. But the pointed nose was designed to droop, so it can be lowered at slower speeds. For take-off and landing, the 'droop snoot' is put right down so that pilots have a clear view ahead.

DE HAVILLAND COMET

The world's first jetliner, the Comet, started flying regularly in 1952. Its first scheduled flight was from London to Johannesburg, South Africa, with five stops on the way. The Comet took 12 hours off the previous flying time on this route. But between 1952 and 1954 Comets were involved in a series of crashes. Tests showed that the fuselage suffered from a problem known as metal fatigue. After four years of improvement, a new, safer Comet took to the air. The aircraft was powered by four de Havilland Ghost turbojet engines which were built into the wings to make the aircraft as streamlined as possible.

LEARJET

Executive aircraft are small jetliners for business people, sports stars and others who can afford to fly them privately. They are sometimes called 'bizjets' (or business jets). This Learjet is just a quarter of the length of a Boeing 747. It has room for two pilots and nine passengers. Some wealthy owners have the cabin of their executive jet specially designed to suit their needs, with armchairs, desks or computer workstations.

MEGA SMALL

One of the smallest bizjets, the Cessna 525 Citationjet, is just 12 metres long. It has room for two pilots and six passengers.

BOEING 747

The first test flight of a Boeing 747 was made in 1969 near Seattle, USA, where it was built. The giant jumbo made its first passenger flight a year later, flying in the colours of Pan American Airways from New York to London. Over the next seven years, 747s carried more than 134 million passengers all over the world. This Boeing 747 can fly for 14,630 km without needing to refuel. It cruises at a speed of 980 km/h.

MEGA SIZE

The Boeing 747-400 is 70 metres long, which makes it more than 10 times longer than the Wrights' Flyer. The jumbo's huge baggage hold, beneath the two passenger cabins, holds up to 3400 pieces of luggage. These can be loaded or unloaded in just seven minutes.

WHIRLYBIRDS & AIRSHIPS

When people first dreamed of flying, they probably thought of machines like today's helicopters. The great thing about helicopters is that they can fly in any direction – forwards, backwards, sideways or straight up. They can even hover in one place.

VERSATILE 'COPTERS

The first practical helicopters were developed in the late 1930s, and since then they have become an essential part of the flying world. Landing spaces called helipads have been built on top of many skyscrapers, lighthouses and oil-rigs. Small whirlybirds are very manoeuvrable, while giant choppers are strong lifters and are widely used in industry and as military aircraft.

The pilot uses a collective stick to make the helicopter go up or down, and a cyclic stick to change direction. Both sticks work by changing the pitch, or angle, of the rotor blades.

MEGA LIFT
The Boeing Vertol Chinook twin-rotor chopper is big and strong. This heavy-lift model can carry up to 55 passengers and lift huge weights such as army tanks.

TG-WIK

Helicopter Rescue

Helicopters can land almost anywhere, but their greatest advantage to the world's rescue services is that they can hover in one place. This means they can be used for the most dramatic rescues, such as lifting sailors from sinking ships, saving climbers trapped on cliffs and mountains, or rescuing people cut off by floods, fires and other natural disasters. Lines can be lowered from the aircraft to hoist up victims in harnesses. Helicopters are also used by the emergency services as air ambulances.

The two rotor blades of the Bell Jetranger (below) are driven by the engine. They whirl round like a propeller and give both lift and thrust.

While hovering, helicopters can spin so the pilot can look in any direction.

The tail fin at the end of the boom acts as a stabilizer and a rudder. The small tail-rotor stops the helicopter turning round in the opposite direction to the spin of the main rotor blades. It also acts as a rudder.

The landing skids are sometimes replaced by wheels or floats.

THE FIRST CHOPPERS

The first chopper to fly successfully never went beyond prototype stage. It was built in 1936 by Frenchman Louis Breguet and had two rotors, with an open framework fuselage. This hélicoptère flew for over an hour. Three years later, the Russian-born American Igor Sikorsky invented a better, single-rotor machine, which included a tail-rotor. By 1944 the Sikorsky R-4B was in full production.

MEGA WHIRL
In 1996, Ron Bower and John Williams of the USA took off from London in a Bell helicopter. They returned 17 days later, having whirled all the way around the world.

SKYSHIP

Modern airships are filled with helium gas, which is safe because it cannot burn or explode. They do not have a rigid structure, but keep their shape because of gas pressure. They are popular for advertising, aerial filming and special events. The Skyship 600 normally cruises at 55 km/h at a height of 6,000 metres. Its two propellers are driven by Porsche engines, and it can stay in the air for up to 50 hours without refuelling.

MEGA DIRIGIBLE
The Skyship is a dirigible airship, which means that it can be steered. The four control surfaces near the back can be moved by the pilot. The propellers are in swivelling ducts, which turn to help with take-off and landing.

MEGA FACT
The Skyship 600 carries up to 13 passengers. The overall length of the airship is 59 metres.

HINDENBURG

The German *Hindenburg* was the largest airship ever built. It had an aluminium alloy frame and was a giant 245 metres long. The gondola carried up to 70 passengers, and the four diesel engines gave it an incredible top speed of 140 km/h. The *Hindenburg* first flew in 1936 and began regular transatlantic flights. It had one big problem, however. This airship was filled with hydrogen gas, which burns very easily.

On 3 May 1937, the airship burst into flames near its landing dock in New Jersey. The *Hindenburg* burned out in 32 seconds, killing 36 people. It was not the only hydrogen-airship disaster, and the great airship age of the 1930s soon ended.

BREITLING ORBITER

The *Breitling Orbiter 3* is an enormous mixed balloon. This means that it has a cell of helium gas inside a large envelope of hot air. Helium is lighter than air, and hot air rises, so the combination is very effective. The air is heated by gas burners. In March 1999, Brian Jones of Britain and Bertrand Piccard of Switzerland became the first humans to fly nonstop around the world in a balloon. Their Orbiter flew for just over 19 days and covered almost 43,000 km. It measures 55 metres in height with a total weight of 8 tonnes (that's heavier than a Learjet!). The Orbiter's enclosed capsule contains a bunk for one of the two pilots to sleep in, a water-heater and a toilet.

In an emergency, such as landing in strong winds or in the sea, the balloon can be released from the gondola capsule.

Full of Hot Air

The hot air for hot-air balloons is made by burning liquid propane gas. Balloon pilots control their height by heating or cooling the air in the balloon. But they cannot control direction, except by looking for air currents blowing in particular directions. Ballooning has become a very popular sport and balloons now come in more and more bizarre shapes, like this motorcycle!

AIR SPORTS

There are all sorts of air sports, involving many different kinds of flying machines. Most are done just for the fun of it, but there are also competitions, based mainly on style, speed or distance covered. Some of the craft have engines, but others simply glide along on the breeze.

MODERN GLIDER

MEGA PAPER PLANE
In 1970 a full-size glider was built at Ohio State University, USA, using only paper, glue and masking tape. The paper plane and its pilot were towed into the air by a car and flew at a speed of 96 km/h.

The most difficult part of flying a glider – a plane with no engine – is getting airborne in the first place. The glider is either pulled along on a long cable by a car or a winch on the ground, or it is given a tow into the air by a small powered plane. Once aloft, pilots try to get a lift on warm currents of air called thermals.

MICROLIGHT

Microlight and ultralight aircraft are the smallest powered planes. They carry up to two people, and many are assembled from a kit before use. This model has a fixed wing, while other, smaller microlights have a flexible wing like a hang-glider. Some have wheels, while this model takes off and lands on water.

Wing Walking

Wing walkers really know what it is like to fly like a bird! They bravely stand on the wing while an aircraft is in flight, attached by a lifeline in case they lose their balance. The world record for the longest wing walk stands at more than three hours.

Aerobatics

In the sport of aerobatics, pilots in single-engined light aircraft are judged on special moves such as loops, spins and rolls. At air shows and other events, display aerobatics by jet aircraft are popular with spectators. The Red Arrows (left) are a world-famous display team who never fail to thrill with their amazing formation flying.

HANG-GLIDER

Hang-glider pilots lie in a harness beneath a large kite-shaped wing, or sail. They hold on to a control bar, and use this to shift their weight and steer the craft, following thermals when they can. To take off, pilots run into the wind on a hill or cliff-top. Competitions are judged on distance and speed, but most hang-gliding is done just for the experience of flying like a bird.

AIR TECH

Today's inventors and engineers make sure that aviation keeps changing. Modern developments include greater use of computer technology and new sources of flight power such as solar energy. Aircraft and airports get bigger and more efficient, in attempts to make flying more comfortable. We can only imagine how things will change in the next century of powered flight.

MEGA AIRSPEED
The world airspeed record is held by a Lockheed SR-71A Blackbird jet, which flew at an incredible 3,529 km/h.

BELUGA AIRBUS

The Airbus Super Transporter A300-600ST Beluga not only has one of the longest aircraft names, it is also the world's most spacious airliner. Its huge, bulbous cargo compartment is most useful for carrying other aircraft parts. The Beluga (named after the white whale of the Arctic) can carry a load of over 45 tonnes.

Kansai Airport

This supermodern airport stands on a man-made island in Osaka Bay, Japan. The island, which took five years to build in the shallow bay, is 4.5 km long and 1.25 km wide. It is connected to the mainland by a long, two-level bridge, with railway lines on the lower level and a road on top. High-speed boats also reach the airport from the port of Kobe in 30 minutes. The airport's terminal, made of curved steel and glass, is designed in the shape of an aircraft wing.

HELIOS SOLAR WING

Helios (named after the Greek god of the Sun) is a solar-powered 'flying wing' aircraft being developed by NASA in the USA. It is flown by remote control by a pilot on the ground, and powered by 14 propellers driven by electric motors. The motors can be powered by batteries, but will eventually be driven by solar energy collected from the top side of the wing. With a wingspan of 75 metres, Helios has a length of just 4 metres!

MEGA FLIGHT

The aim of the Helios project is for the plane to fly for at least four days non-stop at a speed of up to 40 km/h. Once the solar technology is ready, it should be able to fly continuously for up to six months at a time! During the night, the engines will use energy stored during daylight.

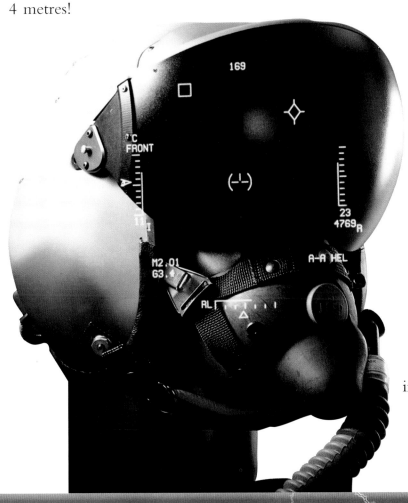

HMDS

Modern helmets for fighter pilots have displays projected on to them. This means that the pilot can look outside the cockpit, rather than down at aircraft instruments, while information is shown inside the visor. The system is called HMDS – Helmet-Mounted Display and Sight. It can also be used to measure the pilot's line of sight, so that he can aim weapons by looking at the target. Other similar systems are used to display information on the cockpit shield in front of the pilot.

GLOSSARY

AERODYNAMICS
The science of shaping machines to slip easily through the air. Smooth, slim shapes are better than boxy shapes.

AILERON
A hinged flap on an aeroplane's wing that turns up or down to make the plane bank and turn.

AIRFRAME
The whole structure of an aircraft, excluding the engines.

AIRLINER
A large passenger aircraft.

ARTICULATED
A vehicle that is capable of bending in the middle.

BIPLANE
An aeroplane with two sets of wings, one above the other.

BOAT
A small, open craft without any deck.

BOGIE
A group of wheels forming part of the undercarriage of a train.

BOW
The narrow front end of a ship, pointed to cut

cleanly into the water.

BRAKE HORSE POWER (BHP)
A measurement of an engine's maximum power output.

CARBURETTOR
Instrument in a vehicle for mixing fuel and air into a combustible vapor.

CATHODE RAY TUBES (CRT)
Visual display monitors used by pilots.

CHASSIS
The structural frame upon which a vehicle is built.

CHOPPER
A slang name for a helicopter.

CLASS
A category of locomotives built to a specific design.

CLUTCH/THROTTLE
A device in a vehicle that connects and disconnects the wheels from the engine, enabling the gears to be changed.

COCKPIT
The cabin at the front of an aircraft where the pilot and crew sit.

COUPE
A two-door, hard-top passenger car that seats up to four or five people.

COUPLED WHEELS
The train's driving wheels together with the wheels joined to them

by the coupling-rod. This arrangement enables the power to be spread over several wheels, reducing slip.

CRADLE
Motorcycle frame which places the engine between two frame tubes.

CRANKSHAFT
The part of the engine in a vehicle which changes the linear movement of the piston into rotational movement.

CUT-OFF
The point in the train's piston stroke at which the admission of steam is stopped.

DIRIGIBLE
An airship that can be steered.

DISC BRAKE
A brake which has two pads that grip either side of a metal disc.

DISTRIBUTOR
Ignition system device on multi-cylinder engines that send the high-tension spark to the correct cylinder.

DOGFIGHT
Close combat between fighter planes.

DRAG
The force caused by the resistance of air that has to be overcome for a plane to fly, or the action of water against the hull and propeller of a ship that slows it down.

DRIVESHAFT
The shaft that transmits power from the engine to the propeller in a ship. Also called the propeller shaft.

ELEVATOR
A hinged flap at the tail of a plane that turns up or down to make the plane go up or down.

EXHAUST
The part of an engine through which wasted gases or steam pass. It ends with a silencing unit, which reduces noise.

FAIRING
A front enclosure to improve a motorcycle's aerodynamics, or the rider's comfort.

FLANGE
A lip on the metal wheel of a train, which keeps it on the tracks and guides it around corners.

FRAME
The structure of plates or girders that supports the boiler and wheels.

FUSELAGE
The main body of an aircraft.

GAUGE
The width between the two rails on a railway track. In Britain, North America and most of Europe, the gauge is 44 inches.

GIRDER FORKS
A common form of front suspension on early machines. The front wheel is held in a set of forks which are attached to the steering head by parallel links.

GLIDER
A plane that flies without the use of an engine.

HELIPAD
A landing and take-off area for helicopters, often on the roof of a building.

HORSEPOWER
A unit used to measure the power of engines (which used to be compared to the power of a number of horses).

HYDRAULIC
Worked by liquid. Liquid pumped to the cylinders moves pistons in or out to move a machine's parts.

HYDRODYNAMICS
The effects and forces produced by and on water when objects are moving through it.

IGNITION
An electrical system that produces a spark to ignite the fuel/air mixture in a gasoline-fueled engine.

KNOT
One nautical mile per hour, or 1.85km.

LIFT
The force that pushes a plane up into the air.

GLOSSARY

MARQUE
The brand name of a car manufacturer. Rolls Royce, Ford, Chevrolet and Lamborghini are just a few well-known marques.

MEGAPHONE
A tapered performance exhaust.

MONOPLANE
An aeroplane with a single set of wings.

NAVIGATOR
A person who plans and directs the flight path of an aircraft.

PLUNGER
Rear suspension system where the axle is mounted between two vertical springs.

PNEUMATIC
Worked by air pressure, or containing air.

POWER STEERING
In a vehicle, this makes the steering wheel move more easily than a manual steering system.

PRE-UNIT
Engine and gearbox constructed in separate units, common on older machines.

PROPELLER
A set of turning blades driven by an engine that push a plane through the air; also, a shaft, formed in the shape of a spiral, turned by the engine to drive a ship.

RADAR
An instrument that uses radio waves to measure the distance to an object and its speed and direction.

REVOLUTIONS PER MINUTE (RPM)
A unit of measure used to express the rotational speed of an engine.

ROADSTER
An open-top car, especially one seating only one or two people.

RUDDER
A flat plate hinged to the stern of a ship and used to steer; also, a hinged flap at the tail of a plane that can turn to change the direction in which it flies.

SHIP
Generally, an ocean-going vessel with a deck.

SHOCK ABSORBER
A hydraulic suspension component that absorbs energy "shock" and so contributes to a smoother, more controlled ride.

SLIDE VALVE
A valve for controlling steam admission and exhaust.

SONAR
A device that detects the location and what an object is underwater by using sound waves.

STABILISERS
Fins projecting from the sides of the hull to help keep a ship steady.

STREAMLINED
Designed with a shape that slips easily through the air.

SUPERCHARGER
Device for compressing the engine's incoming charge.

SUPERCONDUCTING
Having no electrical

resistance. In metals, this occurs when they are cooled to very low temperatures.

SUPERSONIC
Flying faster than the speed of sound.

SUSPENSION
The series of springs and dampers on the underside of a vehicle. The suspension allows the vehicle to travel more smoothly over bumps and uneven surfaces.

TAILPLANE
Fin, rudder, and elevators of an aircraft.

TANK LOCOMOTIVE
A locomotive that carries its fuel and water in bunkers and tanks attached to the main frame, not in a separate tender.

THIRD RAIL
A length of rail built beside the tracks that transmits electric power to the engine.

THROTTLE/CLUTCH
Device that controls the quantity of fuel or fuel/air mixture entering an engine.

THRUST
The force that drives ships forward, provided by the turning action

of the propellers, which throw a powerful surge of water backward; also, the force that pushes an aeroplane through the air.

TORQUE
The maximum amount of force supplied by an engine at a specific speed.

TRACKING
A term used to describe the locomotive's ability to negotiate a curved or irregular track.

TRANSMISSION
A mechanism in vehicle that includes the gears, linking the power produced by the engine to the drive wheels.

TURBINE ENGINES
High-speed engines that work like the jets that power planes.

TURBOCHARGER
A compressor which boosts the engine's intake pressure. In low gears, more torque is delivered to the wheels, improving the car's road-holding ability.

TURBOFAN
A jet engine with a large fan at the front.

TYPE
A category of locomotive conforming in function and basic layout, including wheel arrangement.

UNDERCARRIAGE
The wheels or other structures beneath an aircraft that support it on the ground.

UNIT CONSTRUCTION
The construction of the engine and gearbox within the same casings.

V-TWIN
An engine layout in which the cylinders are placed in a "V" formation.

WINGSPAN
The distance between the wing tips of an aircraft.

WHEEL ARRANGEMENTS
Steam locomotives are often classified according to the White system of notation. Wheel arrangement can be front wheels, driving wheels and rear wheels. For example, a "4-6-2" has four front wheels, six driving wheels and two rear wheels. The German system of notation only counts the wheels of one side, so the above example would be "2-3-1."

INDEX

A

aerobatics 151
aircraft 126–153
airports 135, 152
airships 148
Albion vehicles 109
Alcock, John 133
amphibious vehicles
  cars 99
  trucks 118
Ariel Square Four 66
armored trucks 118
Aston Martin
  DB5 97
  DB7 Vantage 97
Atlantic Ocean, crossings
  47, 133
Austin Healy Sprite 90
Autoped 76
Avro Lancaster 140

B

balloons 149
Bandit 114
Bellini 750 Sei 76
Bell Jetranger 147
Beluga airbus 152
Bennie, George 27
Best Friend of Charleston
  13
Big Boy 15
Bigfoot 93, 112
big rigs 110–111
Blériot Type XI 132
Blue Riband 40, 41, 42
BMW
  Dixi 85
  Isetta 98
  R1200 C 64
Bobcat 75
Boeing 247 136 747
  jumbo jet 142–143,
  145
  Vertol Chinook 146
Bohmerland 74–75
Botnica (ship) 55
Breitling Orbiter 149
Brough Superior SS100 67

Brown, Arthur W. 133
Brunel, Isambard K. 14
bubble cars 98
bulk carriers 47
"bullet" trains 33
buses 116

C

cable-laying ships 52
cableways 28
Cadillac 86
  Model 30 84
  Sedan de Ville 87, 88
  V-63 85
Carolina Crusher 114
cars 78–101
Caterpillar 116
Cayley, Sir George 128
Centennial 17, 19
Cessna 525 Citationjet
  145
Channel Tunnel 30, 32
chauffeurs 88
Chevrolet Corvette 91
Chrysler
  CCV 101
  Jeep Cherokee 124
Citizen's Band Radio 105
Class 58 locomotives 21
Cleveland (ship) 40
compasses 38
Concorde 144
concrete mixers 118
containers 46, 47
cranes, mobile 121
crane vessels 53
cruise ships and liners 37,
  38–45
Cugnot, Nicholas 11, 106
Curtiss, Glenn 70
Cushman Model 52 77

D

Daimler, Gottlieb 61
Daimler-Benz F300 Life-
  Jet 100
de Havilland Comet 144
Deltic 20
diesel, trucks 105
Docklands Light Railway
  21
double-deck rail cars 19,
  23
Douglas DC-3 134–135
"driverless" trains 21
dumper-trucks 121

E

Earhart, Amelia 137
Easy Riders 63
Edison, Thomas Alva 37
Egyptians, ancient 39
ejector seats 153
engines 105
  diesel 17, 18, 37, 50,
  105, 108, 110
  four-cycle 80, 81
  gas turbine 45
  jet 125, 139, 143
  steam 9, 43
  turbine 15, 24
  V8 105, 111
Eurostar 32
Evening Star 8
Explorer of the Seas (ship)
  45
Exxon Valdez 49

F

Ferrari F40 94, 96
fire trucks 119, 120
fishing ships 48
factory 46
FlareCraft 54
flight, aircraft 128, 129
flight deck 129
Flyer 130, 131
Flying Banana 135
Flying Hamburger 18
Flying Scotsman 14
Foden vehicles 109
Ford
  Explorer 125
  F-Series 125
  Model T 82, 84
  Mustang 92
  Super Duty trucks 114
Ford, Henry 82, 83
four-wheel drive 93,
  122–125
Freightliners 110
funicular railroad 28

G

garbage trucks 121
gearboxes 105
gliders 150
golf carts 75
goods trains 27
GPS systems 111
Grand Princess (ship) 39
Great Western, SS 44
ground effect 55

H

Handley Page HP42 137
hang-gliders 151
Harley-Davidsons 62–63,
  68–69, 73
Harrier Jump Jet 141
helicopters 146–147
Helios solar wing 153
Hiawatha Express 25
high-speed trains 18,
  22–25, 33
Hindenburg 148
HMDS 153
Holt, Benjamin 116
Honda Gold Wing
  Aspencade 65
Hummer 123
Humvee 123
hydrogen-fuelled cars 100,
  101

I

ice-breakers 55
Indian Chief 65
Intercity 125 18
Intercity Express 24
iron boat, first 42

J

Jaguar, E-type 86, 90
Jahre Viking (ship) 45, 54
jet aircraft 142–145

K

Kent (ship) 36
Kenworth trucks 120
Knievel, Evel 72–73

L

Lacre vehicles 107
Lamborghini Countach
  96
Land Rover Discovery
  124

Learjet 145
Lenin (ship) 55
Leonardo da Vinci 131
Leyland vans 108
Lilienthal, Otto 132
Lindbergh, Charles 133
Lockheed Constellation 136
Lockheed F-117 Nighthawk 141
locomotives
 diesel and electric 16–21
 steam 8–15, 20, 25
logging trucks 120
Lusitania (ship) 43

M

McLaren F1 94, 95
maglev trains 30, 31, 32
mail, by rail 23
Matchless G3L 67
Mauritania (ship) 40, 41, 43
Mercedes-Benz 300SL "Gullwing" 89
Messerschmitt M2 262 139
Michaux-Perraux 60
microlights 150
Mikoyan MiG-25 Foxbat 141
military aircraft 138–141
military trucks 118
Moller M400 Skycar 101
monorails 26, 27, 29
monster trucks 93, 112–115
motorcycles 56–77
muscle cars 92–93

N

NECAR 4 100
Ner-A-Car 77
Normandie (ship) 39, 40
Normand Pioneer (ship) 53
Norton Commando 66
nuclear-powered ships 50–51, 55

O

oil
 spills 48, 49
 uses 49
Otto Hahn (ship) 50, 52
overhead railroads 26–29
Overkill 113

P

Pacific Mallard 25
paddle steamers 51
Panama Canal 41
Parsons, Charles 43
passengers, train 15
Peel P50 99
Pendolino 33
Plymouth Roadrunner 93
Porsche 911 97
Puffing Billy 13
Pure Adrenalin 114

Q

Qinghai-Tibet Railway 29
Quasar (motorcycle) 74
Queen Elizabeth (ship) 38
Queen Elizabeth 2 (QE2) 41, 45
Queen Mary (ship) 44

R

racing, truck 114, 115, 124
radar 54
radio, Citizen's Band 105
rapid transport systems 31
Rayborn, Cal 69
"readymix" trucks 118
record-breakers
 balloon 149
 hang-glider 151
 motorcycle 73
rail 22–25
recovery trucks 120
recyclable cars 101
riverboats 51
RM Class 4-6-2 14
road trains 110, 111
Robosaurus 115
Rocket 11, 12
Rokon Trailbreaker 71
Rolls Royce
 Camargue 87
 chauffeurs 88
 Silver Spirit 88
Russia, The 22

S

salvage vessels 49
Savannah, NS (ship) 52
Scania 105, 111
 fire trucks 119
scooters 77
Shinkansen trains 33
ships 34–55

Sikorsky helicopters 147
Sinclair C5 98
Sirius (ship) 44
Skyship 148
Skytrains (Skytroopers) 134
Snake Bite 113
solar power 153
Sopwith Camel 138–139
space shuttles 120
specialized trucks 116–121
speed limit, car 10, 85
Stanislav Yudin (ship) 53
steam power
 locomotives 8–15, 20, 25
 steam engines 9, 43
 steamships 36, 38, 44, 51
 tricycles 61
 trucks 106, 108, 109
Stephenson, George and Robert 10, 11
Stirling Single 12
Suez Canal 37
Sumner, James 108
Super Duty trucks 114
Supermarine Spitfire 140
suspended railroads 26, 27
Suzuki Bandit 70

T

tachographs 111
tankers (ships) 45, 48, 51, 54
 oil 47, 48, 49
 sails 53
tankers (trucks) 119
Terex Titan 121
TGVs 22, 23, 24
Thornycroft vans 106
"tilting" trains 25, 33
Titanic (ship) 42, 43
TorqTrac4 123
Torrey Canyon (ship) 48
tracks, railroad 31
tractors 110, 116
trains 6–33
trams 19
Transrapid system 32
Trans-Siberian Express 22
Trevithick, Richard 11, 106
"Trial, The" 42

Triumph
 T509 Speed Triple 70
 X75 Hurricane 64
Truck Fest 117
trucks 102–125
tugs 47, 49
turbines
 gas 45
 steam 43
turbofans 143
Turbomotive 4-6-2 15
two-wheel drive 122

U

Ultra Avenger 71
underground railroads 20
Union Pacific 17, 19
United States (liner) 42

V

Vespa 150 74
Vickers Vimy 133
Volkswagon Beetle 91
VTOL aircraft 141

W

wheels, fifth 125
Whittle, Sir Frank 139
WIG craft 54
Wilkinson, John 42
Williams (motorcycle) 76
wing walkers 151
World War I, aircraft 138
World War II
 aircraft 139
 motorcycles 76
Wright brothers 130, 131
Wuppertal Schwebebahn 26, 28

X

X-2000 tilting trains 25
XPT trains 18